# MELTDOWN

## By

# RICK TUTTLE

**ISBN 978-1-7341927-5-9**

All Scripture quotes are from the King James Bible except those verses compared and then the source is identified.

Address All Inquiries To:
THE OLD PATHS PUBLICATIONS, Inc.
142 Gold Flume Way
Cleveland, Georgia, 30528
U.S.A.
Web: www.theoldpathspublications.com
E-mail: TOP@theoldpathspublications.com

# DEDICATION

I would like to thank my wife, Robin, and children, Christine and Deanna, for encouraging me to write this book.

Thank You Ron and Peg Hardy for the use your vacation home to find a place to write without distraction.

Thank you Patty Primo for your many hours of review and suggestions.

Most of all, thank you Lord for giving me eternal life though Jesus Christ.

# TABLE OF CONTENTS

# PROLOGUE

As his wife Natasha peeked into the church, she found her husband at the front of the church, kneeling down but looking up, as if speaking to someone. As she listened, it sounded like Zain was accepting instructions. To anyone else that may seem somewhat odd, but not for Natasha. There were numerous occasions when she had found her husband in such a deep conversation that he was not even aware of her presence. She listened for just a moment but was certain she heard him say, "Yes Lord, I understand, but others won't. Yes, I will do as you say and not worry about what the opinion of others may be."

Sometime ago her husband, and the pastor for many, had determined that a closer walk with the Lord was not only possible, but necessary for the pastor of a church, regardless of how big or small it may be. While being the pastor of a country church was not his first choice, Zain found himself satisfied to be where the Lord wanted him without consideration of the personal cost. Most men who are called to pastor have dreams of a big church near a city of sufficient size as to feel as though his work is never done. However, when a man is called to pastor a rural, country church and has visited the same house many times, it is easy to start to believe that he is not making a difference.

At dinner that evening Natasha said, "I came by the church earlier and saw that you were in prayer." Her desire was to get a little information as to the content of the conversation she overheard and her curiosity was heavy in the air. She was just itching to hear what "others" would not understand. That clearly did not include her, for although she was quiet, she had always understood the desire of Zain's heart and had often encouraged him when he felt the weight of being a pastor on himself.

"Oh! You heard that?" It was as if Zain, for the first time in their marriage, had a moment when he was hesitant to share with her what the Lord was doing. "When we finish supper and open the Bible I will show you something that I hope will help explain it," he said. The rest of their dinner was eaten in silence. Although Natasha wanted to press for more, she knew it would do little good and could even be an opportunity for the devil to slip in and cause a division.

As was this couple's custom, sharing the cleaning, Zain gathered the dishes and took them into the kitchen while Natasha dutifully and happily drew the water to wash the dishes. Zain finished wiping the table and dried it with a towel so when the Bibles were laid open they would not be spoiled with food. Zain had not consciously thought on it for some time but it was important to him to handle the Word of God with the right heart and attitude, including making sure that it was not damaged any more than necessary.

With dinner ended and the table cleared, Zain opened his Bible to the desired passage and quietly prayed that the Lord would enlighten their eyes as they read and studied His Word. Coming around the corner from the kitchen, Natasha suddenly had a little feeling pass through her that she could not explain, yet it was as if a familiar calm settled in. She knew that Zain had taken his time to bring this study about and a familiar song just entered her mind and escaped her lips in song; "We have come into this house and magnified the Lord to worship Him, We have come into this house and magnified the Lord to worship Him, We have come into this house and magnified the Lord to worship Him, Worship Him Jesus Christ our LORD!"

Zain looked up, tears falling from his cheeks, and said, "Truly God is good and knows just what to do to make this study special." Now Natasha's heart was really racing but she attempted to keep her calm demeanor while she took her seat. What she really wanted to do was grab her husband and shake him and say, "OK! Enough of the secrets! Cough it up!" but instead she just smiled and sat waiting for Zain to lead, as he should, in their nightly Bible time.

Zain looked at his wife of so many great years together and asked, "Do you remember the time when the Lord began to call me into the ministry? Those moments when the Lord seemed so real like we could just reach out and hug Him? Or the time when we were called to start a church overseas for the Military? That closeness would be hard to describe." Puzzled, Natasha looked at her husband and understood that this was not going to be just an average Bible study, but rather a time when the Lord was going to open up to the both of them so He could accomplish His good pleasure.

Breaking the silence in the room, Natasha cleared her throat as if she were about to say something of great importance but she really had such a dry throat it was difficult for her to speak. "I remember like it was yesterday, and also the time when you were not sure about retiring from the Navy and we spent much time in prayer. The Lord just showed up and confirmed that we were right where He wanted us in our lives and that He had a plan that would one day make sense to us." Zain smiled and knew that his "help meet" was right beside him and would understand what would come next in their Bible study. "Do you remember in Genesis when God spoke to Noah?" asked Zain. Natasha sat quietly and nodded her head to let Zain know she was ready and waiting for this conversation to continue.

"I'm not sure if this is going to make sense to you or not, but, like Noah, who was to build an Ark to save the people of the world from utter destruction, the Lord has told me to do some building. Not to save the world, but to care for my family and help meet the needs of others as He would direct." He paused for a moment to let that statement settle in and to prepare her for what was yet to be said. Zain looked intently into the hazel eyes of his wife and coworker of so many years. She hardly blinked and it was difficult knowing if this was making any sense, but he pushed on saying, "God told Noah to build the Ark with specific instructions, and, like Noah, I have received instructions as well. What God has not done is tell me when to begin, where to build, or how this will be accomplished financially."

Natasha finally blinked and swallowed hard enough that Zain heard it. He was thinking to himself, "It must be hard for her to swallow this story," as a smile swelled up across his face. She just looked at him for a moment and replied, "What?" They laughed for a time, unsure exactly why, but it did help to break the tension in the room. After the laughter stopped Natasha said, "Let me get this straight. God told you to build something and has not yet shown you the when, the where, or the how?" "Yep, that about sums it up!" was all Zain could reply. "OK," said Natasha, "I believe you and am here to support you in any way possible. I heard you say that others would not believe you but I want you to know that does not include me, and I'm sure it doesn't include the other members of our family either."

A familiar passage in the Word of God was in their Bible study for the night. *Proverbs 3:5-6. Trust in the LORD with all thine heart; and lean not unto thine own understanding. In all thy ways acknowledge him, and he shall direct thy paths.* After much discussion about this and all the "what if's" they had as the Lord was helping them start this journey, they ended the time in prayer. "Dear Lord, we are in way over our understanding of what you want us to accomplish, so if it's OK with you, we will just follow your Word and lean on you and not our own understanding. We will follow you even when others may not, and we will accomplish what only you will give us the strength to do, Amen."

# MELTDOWN

# Chapter 1

# Spiritual Preparation

Zain Roberts had always wondered if he could pull the trigger when his gun was pointed at a person, as opposed to a target, being a preacher and all. After submitting to training, passing a background check, having a permit issued, and becoming comfortable carrying a weapon, the question remains as to whether or not one could really pull the trigger when called upon. That question was answered a few days after the fall of all he knew of law and order. It was not an easy question to answer, but he determined that any intentional action toward any person that would threaten the well-being of his family, including his church family, would be cause enough. Being a pastor in this day and age was not easy and yet here he was. Zain knew what was coming and making preparation for it was difficult and often accompanied by great criticism, even from the family that he loved so much. Now here he was in a world that you might read about in a science fiction book of apocalyptic proportion.

Time seemed to pass slowly as days turned into weeks and weeks into months. Zain recalled the days when it seemed as though a year would go by and many people would make a comment about time flying. "Busy" would be the excuse many used to not pay attention to the little things in life that truly carry value. Values change quickly when work is defined as a day of foraging for food. Water was not the real issue, as most science fiction stories would depict. He had put in a new well one year before the "meltdown" (as most have come to call it) and with the help of the self-contained power plant there was sustained power adequate to provide for the household needs. The key in this style of living is not to flaunt your preparation accomplishments, lest others would see and act out of desperation or greed to take what does not belong to them.

Food was not an immediate emergency either, but not knowing if life would ever resemble the old normal, Zain felt it important to hunt and fish when he could to supply fresh meat, and not deplete the stored food supply as quickly. The Lord had blessed with a year's supply of freeze-dried foods that was stashed for emergency rations. His family had helped out during a flood in the area and the Red Cross had brought in a lot food. As life returned to normal and the families chose not to depend upon the government but rather depend on neighbor helping neighbor, as it should be, the need for the food supplements dwindled. The Red Cross had already allocated this food and did not want to be bothered with restocking the shelves, so they contacted several of the families that had helped and simply dropped it all in their laps. This was likely a political move. They did not want to appear uncaring and since the amount of food had already been leaked to the press, what could Zain do but thank the Lord and store the food for whatever may come their way? He did, and stored as per the directions, in a dark cool room. Hmmm, who would have ever thought about storage of food? Oh yes, the Lord did! As Zain was building the extra rooms in the secret building project, a storage room was added with just enough space to hold all that food. Imagine that! What God does to prepare His servants!

The most pressing issue they faced was the invasion from the city folk when they realized the government would no longer meet their every need or desire. As a simple preacher, Zain had always preferred country living over city living and now it made perfect sense. The family garden had been planted and they were still reaping the harvest from the previous year with hard work and planning for the old-fashioned act of canning produce. In a few short weeks canning would again be a major task in preparing for the winter months. That is, if there was any garden left to harvest! Protecting family had now been increased to include providing their food and water. Zain had no problem sharing with those in need but watching for the theft of food that was necessary for his family and extended church families by strangers that believed they had the right to take without even asking had become a daily task. What do you tell a man who is scavenging for his family when there appears to be plenty for him to eat and take, but you have planned for the harvest to be used for your family's extended needs?

The first time was the hardest. "Mister, you are on private land without permission and you are stealing what clearly does not belong to you," was what the pastor said. The man's surprise and horror of looking at the barrel of a loaded gun was only momentary because food was so scarce that the threat of death was almost a relief. So what is the "Christian" thing to do? Zain told the man to put it all back, and proceeded to set the man down and began to talk. One conversation that was so easy to avoid in the past was religion, but no more. The preacher was not after religion so much as he was interested in telling a person of their need for Christ as their Saviour. In years past, Zain felt that he always had tomorrow, but now with the days as they were, time is a luxury that many do not have. Each day is a struggle to survive and hard decisions must be made. The Gospel message is not one of forced conversion or even a few hasty words from a frightened man. Clearly a heart transformation is necessary for salvation to be possible. The pastor's job is not to convert, but to tell of the wonderful news of what Christ had done over 2000 years ago on a cross meant to condemn and how God made it a cross of redemption. So, after speaking to this stranger, food was freely given. Zain no longer minced words with anyone, so as to whether he "got saved" or not who knew but God? The stranger listened, asked a few questions, and seemed to be extremely interested in the gift of salvation that God has provided.

The local, state and federal governments had regressed into a vote that was bought and paid for. Over the years the humble preacher saw the warning signs when the news proudly announced that 57 percent of all Americans were accepting some sort of aid for their family needs. That number soon rose to a new record and it was not long after when the bottom fell out of the financial market and the riots that 'would never happen', like those in Europe, did in fact take place. The powers that counted beans knew that, if you had the vote from all that were on assistance, you had the power to hold the highest office in the land. Any person that would call for restraint, or re-evaluation of our entitlement programs, was instantly attacked by the media which in turn kindled the wrath of the people.

No one in this community knew what Hollywood did when the great meltdown occurred. Stories circulated for weeks and families waited with little patience and no restraint. Nonetheless, the hope that the all-powerful government would swoop in and save the day slowly gave way the reality that there was no help coming. This was true throughout this great nation, as day after day passed and hope was replaced with panic and fear. In an economy based on commerce, entertainment, and service, it was only a matter of time before it became impossible to hold up, like holding jello on a nail. There were so many families that had relied on the food trucks for subsistence and they were no longer available.

As Zain watched this he thought it perfectly resembled the "cascade effect." When one service failed the weight was shifted to another, and one by one they fell. Who produces power when there is no money to be made? And what good is money if there is no food to be purchased? The Hollywood that was the hope of this brave, new world of entertainment worth millions of dollars brought no relief to the hungry. And when hungry people walk the streets no one is safe. It was this that caused the government to feel it necessary to fire live ammunition rounds into the crowds. This accelerated the fall of law and order.

The smarter looter sought after canned goods and fresh food items instead of the foolish greed for inedible treasures. The Bible has spoken of these days but the world always thought that America was too big to fall. God has a way of preserving innocent lives even when a government encourages abortion for any reason, making it appear acceptable and even normal. Now a nation stands in judgment with no one to blame but themselves. Many preachers looked the other way, saying nothing and doing less. The political powers made it illegal to approach a woman who was clearly heading toward an abortion clinic. Those daring to press the issue soon found themselves in hot water with the law. Could a nation's judgment come because of sin? Most certainly, but it was the culmination of a culture that rejected God as Lord and Saviour. It was only a matter of time before this house of cards would fall and Zain was a preacher who was looking for the rapture but preparing for the future.

So, to shoot or not to shoot was a real question to be answered, and answer Pastor Zain did! He was prepared. Just a few short days after the great meltdown happened, a man decided to randomly raid and loot homes in the area. No one would ever know what made him choose the Roberts house, but the outcome was certainly not what the man had planned! With a baseball bat in hand, the intruder demanded that the preacher allow him to rummage through the house, and God only knows what else was in his mind. Zain simply said, "No. You will not assault my family and this stops right now." When intruder sneered, "What are you going to do to stop me?" the man of God brought his pistol from behind his back. He was not expecting the intruder's sudden move towards him but he was prepared to respond. A single shot rang out and the perpetrator stopped dead, with a very questionable look on his face. The last words the intruder ever spoke on this earth were, "What gave you the right to shoot?" Zain's answer to that question was simple; "The Bible commands me to protect my family." What the intruder did not know was that being a Christian does not exempt one from protecting one's family.

Since there were no longer any authorities to report the incident to, the now humbled servant had a moment of silence before burying the man in his final resting place in an un-marked hole, or grave, to be more formal. Zain began to wonder how much room would be necessary for this. If this was just the start of this mess, he was sure to be called upon again to protect his family. How could, or would, he stand before the church that he pastors and declare God's love when he must perform such an ugly act? What Zain did not know at that time, was that the very same week, four other families of his flock were similarly required to act. When they came to visit and declare their deeds he shared his story and they all wept. They prayed and asked the Lord for wisdom. The church continued to meet as always but with a new and renewed sense of family.

# MELTDOWN

## Chapter 2

## Intercession

As Zain Roberts knelt in prayer, his heart was heavy and he just cried out, "Lord, I am in such awe as I have been watching you work as only you can. My life has been turned in so many directions that if I did not know you were in charge I could easily be distracted and discouraged. I am in need of wisdom beyond my understanding and yet I know that, during times in the Bible, you helped your men with direction when they did not understand. So Lord, I am not moving from here until I know what my next step is to be." As he knelt quietly, he heard a soft, still voice. It was more like an impression, a presence that could not be defined. Looking around to see if someone was there, he discovered that, as always, he was alone; but the presence was there nonetheless. Zain bowed his head low and simply spoke out loud the words that he had read so many times before, "Speak Lord for thy servant heareth." The calm that followed cannot be described but once again he then knew what would be done. Not knowing how much time that passed that day, the preacher was surprised that when he got up from prayer it was evening. He had started in the morning with prayer time. The day had no doubt passed and to his utter amazement there had been no interruptions with phone calls or visitors that would usually drop by throughout the day.

For a pastor, prayer is not just a requirement, but more a sweet time of rest and close relationship with his God, who chooses to remain a mystery. But it is in those quiet moments that life's plan is so clear. When you live for the time to read your Bible and spend time in prayer there always seems to be great distractions. But this is all the more reason to devote the availability of time to searching the Word of God, not for a message to the people, but rather as a letter from the King. One could only imagine the confusion in his mind when Noah heard the Lord speak to him concerning the building of the ark. No known boats were mentioned in the Bible and yet Noah was directed to build something that seemed to be foreign and unnecessary.

As meaningful time was spent in prayer, imagine Zain's surprise when the Lord directed him to build a house, and not just a house, but one with hidden rooms below the surface. That night, during family quiet time together, Zain told Natasha what was on his heart. Her reply was, "If the Lord is leading then we will follow no matter if we understand it all or not. You are the leader of this house and we follow the man that follows the Lord."

When the money was provided just days after this special time of prayer, there was no doubt in the preacher's mind what was taking place. Several things happened to fulfill the monetary need for this work. The first was the going home of a dear friend and brother. Bob was a member of Zain's church and the pastor had spent much time of late with him as his wife of forty years, Jill, had passed away about a year ago. Bob appeared to fade away without his love beside him. Pastor Roberts and several other church members were called to Bob's simple, two-bedroom ranch home to attend their dear brother's final moments. They were all that were present as the couple had no children, but it was a sweet time and Zain spoke of things to come, when Bob would see Jesus face to face. Bob asked the pastor to sing *What a Day That Will Be* and before he could finish the second verse, Bob was in the presence of the Lord.

The second was a request to be present at the law offices of Smith, Little, and Johnston along with the deacons of the church. They were informed that the church had been bequeathed the house and a sum of cash totaling six million dollars! Imagine the surprise, finding out that Bob had this kind of money. This was a great thing and the pastor spoke of how nice it would be to use the house for visiting missionaries on furlough and for future support. As if this were not a large enough shock, the pastor was personally bequeathed twenty-one million dollars after all taxes were paid with the explanation that this was done because the Lord had directed Bob that this amount be given to Zain three years ago.

Zain asked the lawyer to read it again, in disbelief as he began to weep. When the deacons attempted to console the pastor and tell him that it would be all right, Zain exclaimed, "These are not tears of sorrow, but joy!" He further explained,

"You see, the Lord revealed to me in a dream three years ago that I would be given twenty-one million dollars and that I was to use it to serve the Lord. I had a great laugh and told my wife of the dream. She told me that anything was possible if the Lord wanted it to be."

After this meeting the preacher did not want to tell his wife the news over the phone. He made reservations at a very exclusive restaurant for that evening as well a very nice hotel suite. He also called Natasha's employer and told him that she would be unable to work for the next two days. When Natasha asked him how the meeting went he just smiled and told her she would have to wait until the time was right. At dinner he reminisced about Bob and the modest life he lived and then turned the subject to the dream he had three years ago saying, "Do remember the many nights I woke up with such vivid memories of my dream? I mean, what a time of confusion; I thought I was going crazy having dreams with such specific details." Natasha started to put this together in her mind; dinner at a restaurant they could never afford, reservations for a nice hotel suite, so when Zain got to the part about the dream, she just sat there with a silly little grin on her face. When she mustered a question she asked, "Are you trying to tell me that the Lord did what you dreamed about?" "Yep," was all he could reply. Tears ran down her cheeks as they ate in silence. Not much food was consumed but Zain assured their server that it was excellent. After leaving a very generous tip, the couple made their way to the penthouse suite to relax and talk without interruption.

The following day Natasha gave her two weeks' notice to her employer with no reference to the inheritance. Both Zain and Natasha determined that this was of God and it would not change who they were or what the Lord had called them to accomplish. It simply freed them to obey what He had commanded. Zain, for the first time since being called to preach, could now do so without having another job and Natasha could be a better helpmeet.

The third thing, and part of the prayer time, was the Lord directing in the matter of where to build this "house." Zain had always had a desire to have a piece of land but never seemed to find the right one at the right price. Now before him was land that was by far the best that he had ever seen. Thirty acres with a small rolling hill surrounded by trees in the front of the property and a clearing that pointed to a small pond at the bottom of the hill. There were many standing trees at the back of the property beyond the hill that would become the source of wood for the wood burning stove. All in all, one might think God made this just for the Roberts family. Hmm? Another thing that was amazing was the price. One thousand dollars an acre seemed to be too good to be true until Zain spoke to the farmer that was listing it. He was a devoted man of God and he said that the Lord told him that a man and wife was coming by to look at the land and he was to give this price only to them. They stood and spoke for some time and gave God the praise for his direction.

Pastor Zain was not inclined to speak of the plans he had for the land, but without any prompting the farmer said he also had a tractor, backhoe, and a bulldozer for sale if that might be of any interest to them. Zain stopped in his tracks and enquired as to the price. The farmer looked at pastor Zain and asked him what he needed a backhoe and bulldozer for. This would be the moment of truth; should he tell the truth or should he tell a lie? Of course the answer came easy for the man of God. He had nothing to hide and was sure that the Lord would guide and protect him, so he spoke the truth and gave a broad description of the building that God had called him to build. The farmer stepped back for just a moment and looked into his face, trying to determine if this man was for real or was he just trying to pull his leg. After a few moments the farmer turned to Zain and said, "Son, lets draw up those papers and go to the lawyers. We will need to get an appointment and at that time, I'll give you the price that I would charge for that bulldozer and that backhoe." They shook hands and over the next several days exchanged information and soon enough the appointment was made to meet with a lawyer and sign the final papers.

The appointment did not take long and the appropriate signatures were exchanged along with the cashier's check for the price of the land and, of course, the lawyer's fees. As they were walking out the door together the farmer asked Zain why he had not asked about the heavy equipment? Zain replied, "I believe that piece of business is between you and me, and it is not necessary for anyone else to know the business we conduct." The farmer stood there quietly for a moment and then began to speak. "Mom and I spent much time in prayer these last few days and we believe that the Lord has truly directed your path and the Lord told us to give you the bulldozer and the backhoe." Zain once again felt very humbled and accepted the very generous gift from a fellow believer.

Sunday arrived and Zain and Natasha entered the church as they had every Sunday for so many years. Zain busied himself with a walkthrough of the classrooms, stopping in each one as he did each week and spending a moment in prayer for the teacher and the lesson. Natasha went into the nursery to clean the toys, making ready for the time when little mouths would be eager to chew on them. It was tedious work but needed to be done each week to insure no germs were passed around. When they both had completed their routine, they met again at the front of the church and spent time in prayer.

With services now ready and families arriving at the church, the two servants rejoiced to see such a large attendance. Before the preaching got started one of the church deacons came forward and asked to make an announcement. This was not unusual and Zain waited for the unknown announcement so he could begin the preaching for the day. "Good morning," the deacon said. "You all know the incredible events that have taken place and blessings that have been received." The deacon turned to the pastor and said, "Pastor, we know what the Lord has done and the land that you have recently purchased. We know this is not a money issue but we, as the church, want to pay for the construction of your new home. Again, we know money is not an issue to you but obedience toward our pastor is. We had a secret meeting and agree it is our responsibility for the church to take care of the man of God, so please allow this to go forward and we will receive the blessings from God as we are a blessing to you." With the announcement made he hugged the preacher and returned to his seat, leaving Pastor Zain speechless.

As he looked out at the faces of the flock the Lord had placed in his care, he thought, they are right, money is not the issue but obedience to the Lord, and so, with a humble spirit, Zain accepted the generous gift and turned his attention to the preaching of the Word of God.

# MELTDOWN

# Chapter 3

# Physical Preparation

For Pastor Roberts and his family the real preparation began well over a year ago when they were given the opportunity to build a new house. What others did not know about this humble new house was, that while the basement was being installed, a little extra effort was put into rooms that very few knew about. Not one person, outside of family, had a complete picture of this structure. Who would have ever imagined that a small tunnel led to rooms that were not only a safe haven for foul weather but also a nearly impregnable place where they could spend the nights in safety?

The REAL question was, how do you hide a secret as big as a house? To build a house you must start by acquiring the proper permits, survey the land, mark off the place where the water well will be drilled, and mark off the place where the septic tank will be placed. After all this has been finished and approved, without any knowledge from the world, a secret home is formed beneath the hillside prior to the building of the real house. The key to a successful build is planning and proper material. The building materials are somewhat easy to obtain with little oversight from the government officials. The hard part would be the cement that would be used to make the underground home.

There was a small copse of trees that obscured the new home being built from the road, so when machines were running and dirt was being moved no one would be able to see. In this part of the United States, rural Michigan near the National Forest, there were building projects all around, so this was just another project underway. As long as the traffic was allowed to flow and no one was inconvenienced there would be little difficulty. With careful planning, help from family members in the construction business, and a little extra money, pouring the walls and ceiling was accomplished. Once the underground structure was completed, sealed and buried, the real house could be built and no one would even know about the underground structure. A completely new landscape team was hired and final cosmetics were added so that all would appear untouched until the building of the visible house.

Two separate crews were hired from out of state for the underground home and a local contractor for the home's foundation. With a little money to insure privacy, money no longer being an issue, praise the Lord, the work was accomplished quickly. All this could have been done without help, but at what cost to the body?

A house on a hill is a great way to have a walkout basement. This was done for several reasons, one of which was so the basement would be the family room with plenty of room for games and play space. The basement would appear to be smaller than the house above because the design also included a safe room for foul weather. This room would be twenty feet by fifteen feet and would include an area for storage shelves for storm items like blankets, pillows, fresh water, and a few days' worth of food. These plans were approved by the building inspector and he complimented the fore-planning that had been taken to protect the family. Zain smiled and thanked him with the knowledge that, behind a secret door in the shelving, lay another house that few outside the family even knew existed.

When you have several crews building at the same time a house can be finished in amazingly little time and with little interference from the inspectors. A quick glance at the building from time to time and a thorough inspection for the electrical, mechanical and water supplies, and the building was soon signed off for occupancy. The self-contained hydrogen electrical power plant was a large expense but the savings along with the wind generator and battery supplied power complete with a house inverter was looked upon as groundbreaking. The pastor was asked to share this in a news interview, but because they were trying to remain free from any governmental scrutiny, he graciously declined.

When the plans came to fruition the underground home was just a little bigger than the above ground house. Ample room was necessary for food storage, water storage, a power supply room, and tunnels that could help in any escape and not turn this fortress into a grave. The rooms were large enough to accommodate a family with common areas for gathering during times of meals and prayers. It is funny how little room is needed for relaxation when you are in survival mode. Zain had referred to his experience of living in Europe for a few years while in the Navy. The real priority was the kitchen, simple yet large enough to sit and fellowship with his family.

The door that lead to the completely underground house was constructed and attached by another contractor who was found to be a real enthusiast of what is called "Dooms Day Preparation." To get to the secret house you had to go a special place hidden in the shelf where there was a release switch under a loose board that looked identical to every other shelf board. It could be activated by simply lifting the board. This released a pivoting panel that did not drag on the floor, but seemed to float, as the door swung open to a passage where a safe-like door could be opened only from the inside. The shelf was then closed and a release switch was available from the inside to facilitate any that would desire to leave the safe haven. The safe door remained unlocked while the room was empty but was locked when the family had safely entered. There was no knob to grasp and no place where a pry bar could be inserted to try to force the door open.

When you entered the safe house the layout was simple. There were rooms to the right and left of the center room. Each of these doors was solid wood with dead bolts that anchored into a steel frame. Though this would not stop an advancing intruder, Zain believed it would provide enough time for the family to slip through the hidden panel door located within the closet to the next room and to the next room until they reached the escape tunnel. Once there, they could meet together and choose the next course of action. There was also a gas canister that would deplete the oxygen level within the underground house in mere seconds killing any undesirable intruders if necessary. This was a last line of defense and would be deployed only as they made their way out of the building structure. Each adult member of the family knew the severity of the lever and each would be expected to pull the lever should they be the last one out of the tunnel.

The living space was a little over twenty-five hundred square feet that included rooms for every family member and a kitchen area that also doubled for the common area. There was seating, enough for all that were present, which included chairs around the table and more comfortable seating around the room. The center of the structure was the family room. There was ample room for the kids to play in line of sight of the rest of the family. The kitchen was large enough that it could easily be used as a restaurant to serve forty people at a time. Countertops were plentiful so that all hands could participate in food preparation and distribution. This would not be the place to pull rank and seniority. All would be expected to help with cooking and cleaning of the daily meals. The countertops were not made of any fancy material but with cement, a new innovation, colored and properly installed that would last through extended use with no maintenance needed.

Included were four full bathrooms, complete with tubs for the children and showers for the quick clean up after a long day's work. It was hard to hide the provision that was given, but if the world was living in dirty clothes, then the Roberts family would maintain a vigil so that others would not see them as hoarders of supplies. Just because clothing looked soiled and worn did not mean they could not maintain a clean house and good hygiene. Their daily outer garments would be kept looking just like all the others around them and when they stepped into the home for the night, cleanliness would be a priority. When the water well was dug there were two supply lines attached to the well. One went to the above ground house and the other was directed to the underground structure. With a proper power supply there was ample water and with the tank-less hot water tank, hot water would be plentiful. The septic system and field was below the house so even the underground structure would not have a drainage problem. It seemed tedious to plan with such detail but one never knew how long they may need to stay underground, so to plan for any possibility they could think of was all they could do.

The sleeping arrangements were simple enough but adequate to allow comfort and privacy for every family. For a family with children, Mom and Dad had a separate sleeping room adjacent to the children's room. Each room had an access door through the closet. For married couples with no children a single private room was provided. Fifteen feet by fifteen feet was the size of each bedroom. Bunk beds were provided for multiple children and a lesson on family responsibility was taught from time to time.

One other thing that was tested was the noise level that was produced from the underground house. Surprisingly it was found that no amount of noise was detected from the ground area and they could talk freely, and children could play without risk of detection from above ground intruders.

Fresh air was obtained and circulated from a hidden source and power was generated during the day when wind and sun would charge the power pack conveniently stored in batteries. Power could be drawn for 3-5 days, depending on use, without wind or sun. Installed later, just before the great meltdown, was the self-contained hydrogen unit Zain had read about. A man in Pennsylvania had built a self-sustaining hydrogen collection station and a power generator that runs on hydrogen. Maintenance was minimal and they saw no change in power needs after the meltdown of civil authority and public utilities. The room housing this was accessible from the underground house but there was a large steel door that was used in the event that containment was needed due to leakage of the hydrogen gas. This was also ventilated through a secret ventilation system separate from the living quarters.

The most interesting part was the completely separate electrical grid of the underground house. There was also the entertainment system that consisted of a flat screen TV, an antenna in the attic of the house, a radio to listen for news of interest and stay abreast of the international impact and, of course, a short wave radio that could be listened to but seldom transmitted from for fear of detection.

Skills gained by the preacher through his interests soon became the survival skills that he often thanked God for. Zain had "purchased" a backhoe tractor with a front-end loader. The preacher never applied for building permits for this "little" underground addition in fear that if it were in the public records people may come looking for it. With this being mostly a family affair in construction they were able to complete the structure without undue attention.

A very sensitive security system was installed to indicate if anyone entered the house through the night. Power these days was rare and to flaunt this source to the world would only draw undue attention from strangers who had less hospitable accommodations for their families. They also maintained the battery back-up with small battery voltage lights that would draw little energy to light the rooms as they made ready for a good night's sleep.

There was more to safety than just a safe-like door that when closed would take huge effort to breach. There was also the camouflaged emergency exit in case escape was needed. This emergency exit was inspired by a television show that Zain had watched as a teen, Hogan's Heroes. A tunnel was built with steel pipe that ran out to the edge of the woods behind the house. At the edge of the woods the exit pointed up with a simple manhole access port and then, like in the show, it was fashioned into a tree stump, complete with paint! Let's not forget the small periscope that could be used to look around and see if there was a safe exit without being seen. This too made for great preparation because the tunnel became their own shooting range for the bow and arrow team of the family. Each night there was time to practice at different distances and accuracy was scored when food was brought home for the families of our community. It was funny how, as time passed and more rooms were needed, all the prayer and planning paid off. Planning for growth in the family had been the most difficult part, and, to be honest, it led to much time in prayer. It was necessary to make plans for growth in the event that, as time passed, the family would increase.

It was not long before the path to the secret house could easily be reached by the family members with no lights on so the path would remain a secret. Once inside, the great door would be closed. With the security system activated and the hidden antennas installed they could watch local television for news reports and monitor for any intruders to the property. Each time the family would visit the underground house they would spend time playing games and close the night with a Bible study and prayer. There was no creed to recite but Zain often spent time in the Word of God, looking at verses that spoke of one's conduct toward others. He felt this would be the time to remember relationships toward others before an emergency thrust them into a tight living situation. There was another agenda within this ritual; first it taught the family that the Bible is the authority in their lives, and secondly, an example was set about the importance of the Bible in their lives.

Evenings were called family time, and except for the tired and aching muscles that felt no relief for weeks until the dirt was concealing the underground house, it was a fun time. The preacher thought his family felt that he had gone overboard this time, but they humored him until the task was done. The younger children found this to be a great place to play and run with no one telling them to stop. Now with the family properly looked after, Zain could rest.

The year that followed brought changes to the family when each of Zain's two daughters took a husband. Imagine the surprise when, after the honeymoon, they were given a tour of a house that was kept a deep secret. It was important to guard the closely kept family plans. Now with the in-laws participating, guarding the family was much easier.

Life was normal, whatever that means! When you sit down for a meal and gather for prayer, what do you pray for? Do you pray for a government that is reported by the radio to be in complete disarray? Do you thank God for the good day you had because you did not have to draw a gun on a stranger? One prayer that was common was to seek His grace and wisdom and that all would seek for opportunity to share the real message of forgiveness to the world. Praying for the pastor of the community church was easier for others but not the preacher, for he was that man. Zain's prayer was not for blessings, but that he would make each step a walk of faith. Standing weekly before the small rural church that he shepherded was hard, armed with the knowledge that, when needed, he would practice the role of a shepherd and protect the flock. He didn't believe any man should take pleasure in ending a life, but one should never flinch when confronted with a real threat. There was not a person in the church that condemned the action, but that does not change the feeling of regret and remorse for loss of life. Perhaps it is just that which causes this man to be able to stand, not to brag, but to praise a God who shows His Grace upon all their lives.

# MELTDOWN

# Chapter 4

# The Reset

While the pastor in a little country church was making preparations, completely unknown to him, deep within the White House of the nation's capital, in a little-known room several floors below the house, there was a secret meeting going on. Unknown to the general public, and indeed many White House staff members, there is a safe room large enough to house a full Cabinet meeting should the occasion ever arise. While that occasion had not risen, President Jesse James often used it because of the privacy it afforded him. There was a tunnel that lead to this room from another house that looks like any of the single-family dwelling places several blocks away. This had also been kept secret from the public because it was intended to be used in the event that an emergency escape was needed. It was never intended as an entrance, but the last several Presidents had indeed used it as such to hold discreet meetings when the desire was to exclude the press from the knowledge of who was coming and going.

Seated at the very large table were a few trusted Cabinet members that had been with the President since he served as a Senator from

Missouri. Jesse was a bright young Senator when he was approached by a very left-wing group that pitched a sale; it was time to take America and mold it into the nation they had always aspired for it to be. Jesse was a wild card within the Senate and was known for his flowery speeches that often would include a statement about his family heritage and namesake. The outlaw Jesse James was in fact from the same area but no records have been found to establish the claim that President Jesse James was a direct descendent of the beloved and infamous outlaw Jesse James. He simply claimed that family records were more reliable than government records and he would continue to celebrate his heritage.

The perspiration that was on the President's brow was not from the heat but the information that was being exchanged. There was a scenario being presented with an underlying hint that his participation was not optional. What was so baffling to President James was the intended use of the one book he vehemently rejected and swore that he would never read or quote from; the Bible.

Listening to the Secretary of the Treasury as she read the scenario and the adjoining Bible passage was irritating enough, but to suggest that he would be the one to present this to the people of the nation was almost too much to keep him from exploding. Jesse had always been a strict atheist, or at the very least, an agnostic. Why would he quote from an out of date book that has no relevance for today? Sandy Lemieux continued to read from the Bible, Leviticus 25:13, "In the year of this jubilee ye shall return every man unto his possession." When she finished with the Bible verse she paused and looked at the President.

"What are you telling me? Did I just hear this right? You want me to declare a year of Jubilee? And what exactly does that mean? You know that I don't believe one word that is quoted from "that" book, and you think that I would stand up in front of the nation, and perhaps the world, and try to sell them on something that I don't believe in? You must be out of your ever-loving mind!" exploded Jesse. As his face was turning red from anger and frustration, he noticed a shadow move, and then a man emerged from the dark sound room that he had assumed was empty. It was a man that he had met some years ago when he was a Senator with little experience and a lot of zeal. This man had approached the then Senator Jesse James with a proposal that was not fully understood by the young Senator. When the White House was mentioned, Jesse was all in, no matter the cost. This man was no stranger to the media, for he was reckoned to be the richest man in America, perhaps in the world, should anyone ever track down and add up all known and unknown assets. Donald Maddox remained visible enough that the press did not chase him down and mysterious enough that any inquiries as to who he was, were met with resistance and a warning shot off the bow; just enough to send the message that he would not tolerate any further snooping into his life.

"President James, I don't know if you remember me or not, but we met several years ago in a private meeting," Maddox said. "Sir, how could I forget the day that my life was changed forever?"

replied the President. "I remember you saying that we would never meet again but that things would change in my life with new friends and new goals to be set. I thank you for that day and I would also like to thank you for the financial help you gave to me after that meeting." The stranger gave Jesse a funny look and said, "I have no idea what you are referring to." The Maddox fortune and political involvement was a well-kept and buried secret that few in the world knew existed.

Jesse would never forget the day that he was contacted by the law firm of Smith, Little, and Johnston with the news of an inheritance from a family member that he had never heard of. They sat him down and explained that Sara James/Winifred was a long lost relative on his mother's side that had been married to a business mogul. Since there were no children of the union and her husband had pre-deceased her many years ago, she wanted Jesse to have her total estate, which included several large houses, a very lucrative factory business, and hundreds of millions of dollars in stocks, bonds, and savings. Her entire estate had an estimated value of approximately seven hundred fifty million dollars, give or take a few million due to fluctuation of the stock market. Senator James insisted they check names and social security numbers again, only to be told the search had been extensive and they were confident that he was the right person and the information was not "too good to be true." When he arrived back in his office in the Capital, he found a personal card, with no return address, that was hand-delivered by a courier and addressed to Senator

Jesse James. He opened the envelope and read the card of condolence. There was a personal, hand-written note on the bottom of the card that read "Congratulations and don't mess it up with riotous living!" It was signed "A Friend."

A few seconds of silence passed before President James spoke; "As you said that we would never meet again I am at a loss for words. I am wondering why you are here at this meeting, in this room, especially when you are not on any clearance list that I am aware of. And how could you even know of this room and the secret entrance that you obviously had to take to get here?" he asked Maddox. There seemed to be a bit of surprise on Jesse's part. Donald Maddox popped a piece of gum in his mouth, then said, "I know of this room from previous presidents that I have helped and, if I may be so bold to say, it is none of your business. As for the security arrangements, you could do a little research and find that your personal security in Washington was outsourced many years ago to a very large security company whose employees number into a large army, should one ever be necessary, and is, in fact, owned by me! I already possess any security clearance that would be necessary. I need not explain any further except to tell you that I have access to places that not even the President of this country knows about. While I would like to stay and chitchat, I am a busy man, so I will keep this short. Please have a seat while we talk. I want you to think on what is disclosed for a while before you say or do anything." President Jesse James was not accustomed to taking orders but, for some reason, standing face-to-face with this man, Jesse was compelled to do as he was told.

"Jesse," Mr. Maddox began, "what I am telling you now is not a request and it is not up for discussion so please save your breath. We have been in close contact with many powerful leaders in this "world of equal powers" that exists. For years we have been calculating this very move and believe now is the optimal time to act on our plans. They are rather simple and will be beneficial to the world, as you will see if you will just hear me out and then think about it." He reached into his suit coat pocket and retrieved a cell phone of a type commonly available in all retail stores and known as a burn phone. A burn phone is a phone that is purchased with cash and used in a single activity and can be easily disposed of. He handed the phone to Jesse and told him that he was to call the number on the phone in forty-eight hours to either accept or refuse the task presented to him.

A moment of silence settled over the conversation as the implication of what a refusal would mean began sink in. Jesse got the message and no words were necessary. Mr. Maddox continued with his instructions to the now "puppet president" sitting before him. "As you know the world has been teetering on the brink of a catastrophic financial collapse. The European Union is unable to sustain another nation that cannot pay its debt. America is now over twenty trillion dollars in debt, much of it attributed to former president Barack Obama. Though the blame was placed totally on his shoulders in historical records, the truth is, this was a calculated move with the intention of placing America in a financial crisis that would be impossible to get out of. I do not want any nation to implode, I just want all nations to be equal and America has been the "bully on the block" entirely too long. That is about to change. If you are unwilling, or unable, to see the good that will come from this bold move, Mr. James, we are prepared to call all your National loan notes due in thirty days and the end result will be the same. What will come forth is a new world order. We have determined that the world would be better served if all nations were ruled as one. This was tried through the United Nations once, only to have buffoons who became power hungry and corrupt, try to take over the world. We are not here to take over anything but to restore what we all want, my dear friend, peace and prosperity for all."

This was almost too much to swallow, and President James was feeling sick to his stomach. In fact, he was downright ill and felt as though he could vomit. His simple mind was trying to assimilate all this information. So far, the biggest downfall he could see was the use of the Bible to accomplish the task. The thought, "Why can't this be accomplished without the use of the one book I hate above all?" went through his mind. As Jesse was thinking this through, Mr. Maddox said; "Jesse, you may be asking yourself why we are referring to such an old, out-of-date book that I have never, nor do I ever, intend to read. The logic is simple; the majority of people in the world are not like us here in this room, and they will not understand what we need to do. They are superstitious fools who believe that somehow an unseen God is watching over us all and this God will someday save all his children and they will live happily ever after. We have decided to use this information to our benefit in accomplishing what we know is best for all of mankind on earth."

The President sat up with new twinkle in his eye as he began to see the wisdom set before him. He asked a question without really thinking, "Who is "we"?" The reply was swift and clear, exhibiting no surprise that the President of the United States had asked it. "That sir, you will find out in time, but for now it remains none of your business. If you think that you can ask around to fill in that information, I would advise differently. Others have probed where they did not belong and a shortened life span was the outcome," replied Maddox. Jesse sat back in his chair to digest this information with his smile wiped away and replaced by a serious look.

Donald Maddox finalized his interruption there with a few short instructions. The meeting came to an abrupt halt as the mysterious Donald Maddox rose from his chair with a smile on his face. He knew that he had another country that would follow the plan that was secretly given to him by a stranger some forty years ago. As he rode through the tunnel on an electric cart, his breath was deep and refreshing as he was certain that he would not have to replace another President or further delay what he had planned for so many years. This time he could not, would not, fail.

President James returned to the Oval Office of the White House and cancelled the rest of his meetings for the day. He quickly made his way to the private quarters reserved for the family and closed the door. He was sitting on the couch when his wife, Susan, came through the apartment and stopped abruptly, realizing something was not normal with her husband being in the room. She sat down next to her husband and reached for his hand and said, "Honey, what is wrong? You have more meetings than I can count and you should not be here."

For the next two hours they spoke openly and honestly, asking questions of each other and trying to absorb all that had been said. Susan gave the love of her life a hug and a kiss and reassured him that this was the right thing and that this would solidify his name in history. No more would the name Jesse James be the name of an outlaw. This wonderful name would be remembered as the name of the man that brought salvation to the world in a miraculous way. Could there truly be a God that would set all this in motion to accomplish greatness to this nation?

Jesse returned to the Oval Office of the most powerful nation in the world, at least for today, and began to draft the speech of a lifetime. He called in several Cabinet members that fateful day. He did not disclose all the information to every person, but enough information to accomplish the work that was assigned to them. There were a few who knew the whole secret of the subterranean meeting and they would be the ones to help draft the treaty along with trusted allies. The Congress and Senate would be happy to take credit for what they drafted. The introduction of a new treaty that would alter a nation while insuring the strength and security of our beloved United States, at least in name, would be a news event that could not be squelched, but with the news media on his side, he would have some control.

First they would blame the conservative Christian movement that had gained some strength, but not enough to stop any real momentum for this history-changing treaty. Then, strategically timed leaks about the contents would begin to surface. This would give rise to grumblings, but the end result would be that the people of the nation would gradually, as information was leaked, come to embrace what was inevitable. Lastly, with what would appear as majority support with a little help within the media, a speech would come from the President of the United States.

For the president to be assembled in the Oval Office for what was believed to be the daily cabinet meeting with a few guests was not unusual and went completely unnoticed and unreported. Time for public support would come but today was a strategy meeting with all necessary people who would not question the direction President Jesse James was headed.

"Good Morning ladies and gentlemen," said the President. "I know you are expecting to go through our normal routine but today we are going to take a different direction that should not surprise you. There are forces that have been put in place around the world that are determined to accomplish what we have always wanted, peace. All the details are not yet before us but we have enough to move forward with our part of the greatest event in the history of the world. This is no joking matter. I want to share a Bible verse that is given for this inspiration."

Several members snickered, knowing the distaste President James had for the Bible. As the laughter subsided, President James continued his introduction saying, "I have not read the Bible, but this verse was shown to me and will help explain what we are going to propose to the world, not just the United States of America. Leviticus 25:13 says, "In the year of this jubilee ye shall return every man unto his possession." As President James finished with his pep talk and Bible reading, he opened up the floor for discussion of ideas and strategies that would be needed to accomplish such a task.

The first question was who was going to sell this? Not only to the United States of America, but, to the world? "Well, that part is already underway as I understand it," replied the president. "I believe we will announce this treaty simultaneously to the world so that no single nation will have an advantage over another. I have been selected to introduce this to our people and I am sure we will have ample time to meet the others in this delegation. What we need right now is an introduction to key players in the Senate and House of Representatives to get the official paperwork going forward. That is why you are all here. It is now February, and the election is behind us and no re-election is before us as we are in our second term. This is an obvious statement, but necessary, so that the people will realize there is no political gain for me in this matter and that the best interest of the country is our goal. While this is true, the selling of the event will best be done by key people in the media. I am going to bring in three networks for a private meeting, at which I will have their complete cooperation or they will be excused prior to any information being unveiled."

He continued to expound, saying, "The target date for a "Reset" of the world economy has been set for January 1$^{st}$ of this year. That way no person or country can run up large debts knowing they will not have to repay it. The world debt will be reset on Zero, Zero, Zero One, of January One, Greenwich Mean Time, or as aviators will recognize as Zulu Time. The reason for this is to prevent the possibility of manipulation. What will happen at that time is that computers will register zero indebtedness and every loan or transaction after that moment will be payable as per the terms. So if you had a student loan or a home mortgage loan and it was closed December 31$^{st}$, then your balance due would be zero. If you finalized the loan on January 1$^{st}$ your loan would be in payable per the terms of the contract. The event will be worldwide with all countries participating. If any country chooses not to participate, then their debt will be called effective immediately and all future monetary transaction terms would be cash with a gold standard to back up the currency."

The room was so quiet that the irregular breathing each of them was experiencing could be heard by the others in the room. This silence was broken when a single clap was heard, followed by others, until each person stood and congratulated the president for his brilliant strategy. With the room in an uproar of excitement it was nearly an hour before a semblance of order was re-established. The idea was received with enthusiasm, but the hard part was ahead of them when those pesky conservative party members who cling to the ancient document called the Constitution of the United States got wind of the plan. It would require a fundamental shift in teaching; knowing what was being proposed was, in fact, against the very laws that had been established for centuries. What most Americans did not know is that "IF" a treaty was signed and ratified by the House and Senate it would supersede the Constitution of the United States. With the backing of the people, acceptance of this new deal would be swift; after all, with just the mere mention of free money or forgiveness of all debt, any opposition would be dealt with by the people in the form of a mob. The real opposition would be from those who did not qualify for this unprecedented shift of wealth and debt. There would be a campaign of sympathy but in the end they would come to realize this was the right decision.

The President continued, "We will promote the notion that, although there is a hard and fast line that cannot be breached or compromised without political pressure, the end result will be that the job that you currently have will more than meet your needs because you will not be burdened with any old indebtedness, only that which you have accrued since January 1st." The room erupted again into a cacophony of speaking, one to another, which sounded like a herd of animals running across a field. There was not a single distinct voice, just one large noise. The President leaned back in his chair and looked out the window, basking in the knowledge that he would be thought of as the savior of the financial system of the world, or at least of his little corner called America.

# MELTDOWN

# Chapter 5

# First, The Good News

After what felt like years of work, but actually only taking several weeks, President Jesse James was now standing at the podium ready to give the speech of a lifetime. With so many hours invested and with very little sleep, the weary look and worn-down features of their once vibrant and youthful president was noticed by the press that was invited to this important meeting. For some of the press this was a mere formality. They already knew the news that was coming from the president. For the rest of the unsuspecting members of the press there would no doubt be mixed emotions and reactions.

Unbeknownst to the majority of the presidential press, there would be a time of questions and answers following the speech. Placed strategically within the group of men and women were a select few that were privy to the information not yet known to the world. "Good morning ladies and gentlemen!" the president began, as he cleared his throat indicating it was time for the news to be released. This was not an uncommon scene for President Jesse James. He appeared to like the spotlight and cameras much more than previous presidents. At least once a week he found himself behind the podium speaking to the members of the press. He continued, "I'd like to forgo the usual pleasantries and spend some time with you today giving you some information that can only be described as life-changing."

A hush fell over the room. All eyes turned on the president knowing that the cameras were running, and the audio was synchronized so that every camera would have optimal sound. "Ladies and gentlemen what I'm about to tell you is going to sound extraordinary and unobtainable, but I assure you that the wheels are turning and a unilaterally supported treaty will soon be released by Congress, ratified and ready to implement. You might ask, "What is this treaty?" For many years, our country, and many countries of the world, have struggled to balance budgets, but due to unfair trade practices and huge debt, it appears impossible that this will ever happen. So, for the first time in the history of America, we will be instituting what we are calling a "Reset" program that will allow all participating countries to start over with a clean slate. To facilitate this it will be necessary to choose a date that has already passed. That will prevent people and countries from creating new debt, secure in the knowledge of debt forgiveness. Not only will this "reset" affect our nation's debt, it has been agreed upon through negotiations by all world powers and will be implemented into law. There will be forgiveness of all personal and national debts prior to January 1st of this past fiscal year. Before we have any questions and answers, I would like to announce to you that this is not a new idea. History would show, in fact, that this practice has been used for many millenniums in the Jewish community. We found this truth in the Bible, specifically in the book of Leviticus. Every fifty years there would be a year of Jubilee wherein all debts would be forgiven, all slaves set free, all properties returned to their original owners, and the people of the land would start afresh. We have modified this Bible truth to help you understand and to pass this information on to the public. Let me make myself perfectly clear. There will be no backroom negotiations, the date has been set firm and there will be no loans made with retroactive dates. Any violation of these simple rules will result in the guilty parties being charged and standing before a court of law facing stiff penalties and jail time. There will be several days of briefings so that you will have the most accurate information prior to your release to the public. No doubt this news to some will be refreshing and yet to others will be alarming. Although I cannot tell you how to do your job, I would hope that you will give the legislature ample time to answer your questions, making this a joyous occasion. Celebrating the forgiveness of debt around the world will have a profound impact and I'm pleased and proud to be the one to introduce it to you today. Are there any questions at this time?"

One by one, the planned questions were asked and subsequently answered. To President James' surprise, it appeared that the press received the news with gladness, not remorse or regret. As he stepped away from the podium that he'd been in front of for nearly an hour, he stood in the hallway with the door barely open so that he could observe the reaction without being in the room. What he heard was excitement as each reporter made ready to submit the sound bites provided to them from the White House during this briefing. Satisfied that he had heard enough, the president quietly walked down the hall with his aides into the Oval Office, ready to meet his rigorous schedule for the day.

His first phone call was made from the personal phone that had been given to him by Maddox. It linked the White House's Oval Office to the coordinating office of the worldwide event called "Reset." A familiar voice on the other end of the line, which was simply identified as the "secretary" answered the phone, knowing by the incoming number that the call was from President James. The pleasant voice of the secretary spoke to him and said, "Good morning Mr. President. I assume that you're calling to report that the press release has begun?" "That is precisely why I'm calling, thank you very much," said the president. "I want to report that it was received with excitement and embraced as a job well done. I anticipate few difficulties as the days go by and the news is passed to the people of America." "Thank you so much," said the secretary. "I will pass this news on to the director, but may I also report that you are the first phone call in? With this good news we believe more than ever that we are on the right path for the world! Have a good day sir."

As the phone was set in its cradle, the secretary turned to see the expression on the face of her boss, Mikhail Moretti. He had a single speaker on his desk and had heard the entire conversation from the first phone call of, no doubt, numerous for the day. Unbeknownst to President James, America would be the leader of this movement. If the American people accepted it then the world would embrace the news as well. If the American people rejected it, then President James would become the scapegoat and it would just be reintroduced through other means.

Mikhail Moretti would soon be revealed as the great negotiator of the deal that would change the world. Although a man of great wealth, Mikhail, called Mick by his friends, appeared to live a simple life with no vices or temptations in his life. Born in the European Union, Mikhail's father was one of the richest men in the European and Middle Eastern area. His father and mother never wed, believing that marriage was a tradition that just held people back from truly becoming who they want to be. They met while his mother was attending school in France and working as a servant in the house of his father. Although she was of Syrian background, she carried no baggage of religion with her. They both agreed that marriage was a mere religious institution and that they had no reason to embrace it. As their relationship deepened and Mikhail was born, he took his father's name, as agreed upon. Mick grew up surrounded by servants and people that tended to his every need, yet so often he felt alone, having no friends his own age. His parents had homeschooled him with the finest tutors that money could buy and he graduated at the young age of 16. He was subsequently tutored in the family business. Obviously, he would one day assume the reins of his father's great financial empire.

At the age of 17 he received unexpected news that his father's private jet had somehow lost hydraulic maneuverability and had plummeted into the Swiss Alps, killing both his mother and father. He had stayed behind preparing for a business meeting. Thus began the dark years of Mick's life. During the memorial service he showed little emotion and the employees of his father's vast financial empire were in awe of the strength of this young man.

When at home and out of the public spotlight, Mick was extremely enraged and he lashed out at one whom he had never been told of yet knew in his heart existed; God. During this time of grief, like his father before him, he rejected any authority that this powerless God could, or would, have on his life. Instead, Mick began to seek out other answers and this led to him to finding a companion of unknown origins whom he soon invited to be a major part of his life. This new companion helped through the tough days as he firmly and decisively took control of his father's estate as dictated in his parent's will.

■■■■■■■■■■■■■■■■■■■■■■■■■■■■■■■■■■■■■■■■■■■■■■■■■■■■■■

Reeling with anger at a God he did not know, Mick called out a curse into the air where unbeknownst to him was a listening ear. This unknown invisible creature was neither sitting nor standing but more like floating in the room without taking up any real space. He quietly listened as Mick cursed the very God who gave him life and he was unaware of. The entity's breath was vile and cold and if discovered in the physical world would have the stench of sulfur. With Mick now drawing to a conclusion his rants against an unknown God, the creature that had been invisible now made the choice to show himself in this opportune time.

Mick's house is one of the most secure houses on the planet and it came as a surprise to him when, out of nowhere, this man seemed to appear. The unknown man began to speak with words that he hoped would bring calm to Mick. "Please do not try to contact your guards, I am not here to hurt you but I am here to help you," said the stranger. Mick who was quite startled had to ask the question, "How did you get in here past my guards and security measures?" The stranger replied, "The things that you call security are of no concern to me but I promise you that I am not here to hurt you. I only desire to speak to you for a few moments and after, if you so choose, then I will leave and never return. So let me answer your question; you were cursing a God that you did not know and I happened by and heard you cursing. I am here to help you through your grief and, if possible, to help you find revenge for the death of your mother and father." Mick replied, "That does not answer my question! Who are you and how did you get in here?" "If you must know," said the man, "I am a spirit being and have the ability to be invisible when necessary and visible when called upon. Many eons ago I followed my master in an attempt to become a god and that has left me wandering this earth helping others in times of grief and anger." Mick asked, "So, are you a demon or are you an angel?" "I am many things to many people but suffice it to say today I would like to be your friend. I have not come here to hurt you but to help. I will help you through your grief and in the future, if you should let me, I will help you in your daily life" said the being. Mick said, "As you can see I have been raised in a very wealthy family; my life is secure and I have very few friends so I am not looking for help as you think, I am looking for a friend who I can call upon and speak to as no person on this earth can understand. I will continue with this conversation and allow you to remain without any alarm to my security force and if you are who you claim you are, I look forward to a deep relationship that will help me find revenge toward this God that has caused me so much grief and pain because of the loss of my family."

Mick was curious as to how he should address this new-found friend by name and so he asked, "What is your name and how shall I address you?" The stranger replied, "I have many names that have been given to me over many lifetimes but you may choose one that is suitable for this day and I will answer to that name from this time forward as our relationship deepens." Mick contemplated for some time and then replied, "I will call you Giovanni and as our friendship grows I will refer to you simply as Gee." Giovanni liked his new name and accepted his role in this new relationship. He helped Mick understand that in this world there are two forces, good and evil. What he failed to tell Mick was that in the Bible he would be referred to as the evil, but he instructed Mick that he is the good force and that the evil that prevails upon this world is in fact the one that has caused so much pain. Gee walked with Mick every day for many weeks and gave him great wisdom and understanding into the working and leadership of his new life formally known as his father's world.

Over the next weeks and months, the security force around Mick's house had come to understand that this friend, Gee, had abilities to come and go without their knowledge or understanding. They chose to follow the instructions of their employer and did not seek any further understanding. The new friend indeed was kind to Mick and a sense of peace seemed to reign over the family. Little did Mick or anyone else know that this friend and many others who would be unseen and unheard around the grounds would remain vigilant to the task at hand; the victory that they had sought for many millennial over the one who judged them and cursed them to this earth with no hope of redemption, would soon be here.

••••••••••••••••••••••••••••••••••••••••••••••••••••••••••

Now, twenty-three years later, at the age of forty, Mick sat in his office patiently waiting for the phone calls that he knew would be coming in. One by one, first America, then Canada, followed by Mexico, and then sweeping through Central and South America, they began. The rest of the world would soon follow and over the next two days the "reset" program would have a strong foothold around the globe. Once and for all Mick would show this so-called "God" in heaven that he had no control over the events on this earth. Mikhail would be the one to rule and reign with a rod of iron.

It did not take long for the news from President Jesse James to go out over the airways. Admittedly, this was just the introduction and it would take several days, perhaps weeks, to fully reveal the complete plan and how it would impact America. However, that was not the job of the news organizations. They were only called to report that which others were doing. It did not matter what channel you were tuned to, even cable television networks broke their protocol of uninterrupted television for this earth-shattering news. "We interrupt the regularly scheduled program to report breaking news from the president," said the announcer on the TV. "President James has just announced a treaty that has been negotiated throughout the world and will soon be ratified here in America, that will, in effect, and I quote his words, "Reset" the indebtedness of America and the American people. All Americans are informed to continue to pay their bills until such a time as all the details will be brought to light. We realize that this news appears sketchy at best, but as our news reporters receive new information, we will be sure to pass it on to you, the American people. We now return you to the regularly scheduled program already in progress. Good day."

Of course, the White House had been monitoring all major television channels and they were pleased with the release of the report. They had anticipated some resistance but assumed it would be accepted by the majority of the American people. It was assumed that any dissenters would soon find themselves outnumbered and unable to stop the inevitable. Cheers were heard throughout the White House and the president would soon be going on the road to promote this treaty. Jesse knew that this treaty would affect the world in such a way as to make it the best move America could make.

••••••••••••••••••••••••••••••••••••••••••••••••••

Natasha was busy around the house with her morning chores of cleaning and vacuuming, keeping the house presentable. The TV was on in the background as it often was for the news and noise. She paused in front of the TV when she saw that there was an interruption of the daily program. As she watched, it became crystal clear that her husband had been right and the preparations that they had struggled with for so many months would clearly be the physical salvation of her and husband and their family. She picked up her cell phone and pushed the speed dial number to her husband's private phone. Zain was engrossed with his daily Bible study and time with the Lord but paused when the phone began to ring. Looking at the phone, he saw that it was his wife and was somewhat concerned. She never bothered him during his study time. He answered the phone saying, "Hello sweetheart, what's the matter? You never call me at this time of day!" "Zain," she said, "I know you're studying and that you normally would not want to be disturbed but there was a newsbreak on the TV and I believe it is news that you'd want to hear right away." Although Zain did not have a television to interrupt his study time, it was not hard to open a program on his computer and stream live news events. With a few keystrokes, while speaking to his wife, the computer came to the news station that he trusted for accurate information. He listened as the news was being repeated over the airways and through the cable television station. He completely forgot that Natasha was on the phone. When the newsfeed came to an end she brought his mind back by saying, "What do you think about that?" "Wow!" was the only word he replied. After a long pause he said, "The world is about to change and the Lord has seen fit to prepare us for that change. I am going to spend some time in prayer and then I'll be home and we can talk about this in private." Zain pushed the end button, looked up toward the heavens, and began to thank God for his love, mercy, and provision. He closed his Bible and spent a short time praying before deciding that being with his wife, calling his children, and making preparations, were the most expedient things to do. So, with a heavy heart for the uncertain days before them, he closed his office, locked the church quietly, slipped into his vehicle, and pointed it towards home.

# MELTDOWN

# Chapter 6

# Where Is God

Zain had always preached that living by faith did not include laziness, and although we know our Redeemer will return one day, the question has always been, "When?" Since no man knows the time of our Lord's return it would be a wise choice for all of God's children to look for His return and be preparing for the inevitable. There will come a time when Christians will be shut off from the world and faith will be unpatriotic. As of yet, no law had been passed against a believer in this land but there was a growing unrest toward believers. The media reported with great prejudice that the troubles of this world could be traced to those who will not give up their old-fashioned beliefs and embrace the new law of the land, tolerance. How odd that those calling for tolerance had no intention of giving any, especially to those who stand up and dare to disagree with them.

The first Sunday after the 'meltdown,' Zain's little country church, located in mid-America, gathered together and the first question he heard was, "Where is God?" quickly followed by the second, "When will the rapture take place or have we been left behind?" To tell the truth, pastor Zain knew these questions were not going to be answered with simple answers. He also knew that the Bible has all the answers so it would be necessary for him to find those answers. The answer to the second question was an emphatic, "No, we have not been left behind!" To the first question his answer was simple, "Still on His throne in heaven where He told us He will be."

While standing in the pulpit that Sunday, pastor Zain said, "We were never promised that life would be paradise and to believe that we are exempt from hard times. That would be buying into the great 'American Lie.' The truth is that the world has a great disdain toward God and, as His children, we have often been spared from the tribulation of frontal confrontations. Well, it appears that is changing, and many will pay the price with their lives, being martyred. Revival is not persuading man to be godly, but rather, that man would agree that God is Holy and that He demands the same from His children. So in the middle of hardship we can, and will, find that God is the only stability in an unstable world." A short, but pointed, sermon followed these candid remarks. At the close of the service pastor Zain called for a season of prayer. For the first time in his preaching career the pews were empty and the altar was full. Zain's wife clung to him as they prayed for wisdom and grace.

The families of this little country church agreed that banding together against what was coming would be the best plan. That way they could help each other when they could and protect when they must. The real struggle for Zain was his family, his wife Natasha and two daughters Ann and

Amy. Ann, the oldest, born Antoinette Christine, was born into the Roberts family while Zain was in the Navy and before he called to preach. While Zain had chosen to join the Navy, Ann had been more like drafted into this life and followed where the Navy called and where he was allowed to bring his family. It is a good life experience to live in many places around the world, but it can also be a burden. Where do you call home and where are your lifelong friends? Add to this the wonder and burden of a child with a medical condition and no cure in sight.

There are many difficult things in life a man can bear but when your child is under a weight like that, a father can only call upon the Lord with great faith and ask the Lord for the strength to carry this weight. During the first years of Ann's seizures, Zain stood strong, sure in the knowledge that the Lord would heal her to His glory. But as days turned into months, and months into years, he found himself asking the same question that the church had just asked: "Where is God?" Accepting God's will when his child was so stricken was one of the hardest things he had encountered his life. Then the Lord settled this question for him completely with a verse from the Bible, "My grace is sufficient for thee." With this answer, Zain fell to his knees and thanked the Lord for this struggle. He has yet to find an untrue promise from God's word. This was not always true for Ann, as she continued to ask, "Where is God?" when she suffered an episode. Now with the great 'meltdown' before them it was Ann who stands as a testimony of God's provision and His wonderful grace.

"Dad, if the electricity doesn't come back or the delivery trucks do not deliver to the drug store, what will happen to me?" she asked with concern and fear in her voice. "Well, honey," Zain comforted, "we can only take this one day at a time and ask the Lord for wisdom." She didn't know that her father and pastor had already been on his knees before the Lord with these questions and had already received God's simple reply, "Trust Me." In tears Ann said, "Ok. If the only thing we can do is pray, then I will do just that. Would it be wrong if I asked God to heal my body again? I know I have asked that a lot over the years, but I really want the Lord to direct every part of my life." Zain's reply was choked with emotion, the tears running down his cheeks, "Honey you can pray for anything. That is what the Lord instructs us to do. I just want to remind you that the Lord may answer your request with a 'no.'" "I know Daddy, but I just want to ask Him again," Ann said, also in tears. "Then you pray so and your mother and I will pray also," said Zain.

Like most children, Ann had not always listened to counsel from her mom and dad and while the "I told you so" never came from them, it had surely gone through her mind. Ann had twins from a failed marriage and while that was not a curse, they were a handful! Now, six years old and being homeschooled, Dee Dee and Jessica missed going to school but Ann was concerned that public education was taking a very dangerous direction. Evolution was no longer taught as a theory but as a fact. Reading was no longer taught using phonics but memorization and pictures instead of sounding out words.

Ann had a teenage daughter also, although not biologically. Temperance came with her failed marriage, which lasted only 4 years, due to her now ex-husband having wandering eyes and roaming feet. Temp, as she likes being called, asked to stay with her new family and the only real stability she had ever known. Temperance had proven to be a real blessing to Ann; the old adage was a simple truth; many hands make light work.

Dawson entered Ann's life when, as an over-the-road truck driver, he decided to come home to his family after living in several towns around America. As a Christian he knew it was important to get involved in a local New Testament Church, so he came with his parents to church where Pastor Roberts and his family were serving. Little did he know that he would join the Roberts family, but that fateful day occurred and a friendship grew into a proposal of marriage. What Dawson was not expecting was the tour he received after they returned from their short honeymoon and he saw the family living arrangements and became aware of his assigned duties. He was not one to argue with what God had clearly arranged and he loved the idea of being in this new family with a purpose to serve God.

Temp's love for shooting had caused her to become more than just proficient with a gun. Zain would label her in the expert range. She developed this skill through many shooting competitions and thousands of rounds of ammunition. Hunting is a skill that both she and her best friend, Kairi, enjoyed. Kairi's love was not a rifle, but a bow and arrow. With a few pointers from family members and a lot of time spent practicing, her skill had risen to a level that could match competition notoriety, yet she chose to simply shoot for pleasure without the pressure of scores. She could walk so quietly through the woods that her skill was defined by what she brought home, not for competition, but to help provide church families with meat for their tables.

While Zain did not know how the season of prayer would change life around the Roberts household, Ann's medicine ran out less than a week after their conversation. A call to the pharmacy revealed that there was no medication available, not a big surprise. They said they were very sorry and expected a new delivery any day. This situation had been secretly discussed by many experts and it was agreed that there would be a large number of fatalities around the world because of the lack of needed medication. Though it was never openly discussed, this shortage was not only planned but cleverly executed. As only a politician could verbalize it, "Never let a good crisis get by you." Pharmacies around the world were reporting shortages of most life-sustaining medications. It was not long before the death tolls were left unreported due to the fear and panic, and to prevent attempts of retaliation toward those responsible.

With no medication available, the effects on Ann would come soon, although it would take a few days before the residual medication would be out of her body. What Zain and Natasha feared never occurred. In fact, what took place was nothing short of a miracle. Ann had always loved the woods and shooting the rifle, but when the fatigue of her health condition set in, she had given up on such parts of her life. When her meds ran out, instead of the seizures overcoming her body, the family saw a new life in her eyes. Instead of fatigue they saw energy.

One morning soon after this, Ann asked, "Mom, Dad, I want to go to the woods and do a little hunting. I plan to bring back a little meat for dinner if that is ok with you?" "Sure Ann, but what about your seizures?" Natasha asked. "Mom, you see what has taken place in my body? I am feeling like I have not felt in years. I just want to get out and help with the family needs." On the morning of what should have been one of her last days, Ann simply picked up her rifle and headed out the door. A crack shot at targets; Ann wondered what she would do when an animal was in her sights. She turned with the .22 caliber rifle in her hand and walked out the door. As she walked into the woods alone, just her and the great outdoors, she knew she was not alone. "Dear Lord," she prayed, "I want to thank you for this new gift of life in me. Please help me to shoot straight and allow a precious animal that you have created to come before me that I may provide for my family. Amen." Ann walked for a short distance just as she had in the past but with a new determination. Right ahead was just what she had prayed for with open eyes and an open heart! A rabbit had stopped about 60 feet in front of her. Ann just needed to aim as she always had and shoot like her daddy showed her. She had a moment of doubt and it looked like her nerves would get the best of her. She thought to herself,

"Why am I so nervous? What is the difference between the target and the real deal?" She answered herself in her head, "Nothing; now do what you have asked the Lord's help with. Careful, steady, aim," she thought, "squeeze, don't pull the trigger." Then, "BANG!" As Ann looked through the scope, she saw the little animal fall to the ground. Although it sounds grotesque, a head shot is the quickest and most humane shot. Ann took a moment before retrieving the rabbit, kneeling down for a moment of thanksgiving to the One who gave life. "Lord I want to thank you for your love and I want to thank you for how you touched my body. And Lord, thank you for the provisions you have supplied for my family." As Ann stood up, not more than 25 feet from her was another rabbit. Simply, by the numbers, she thought again, ready, aim, squeeze. "Lord, I thank you again!" praised Ann happily!

• • • • • • • • • • • • • • • • • • • • • • • • • • • • • • • • • • • • • • • • • • • • • • •

"Where is God?" Zain asked that Sunday as the church family gathered together to worship. And worship they did! Many who knew Ann only during her time on medication were having a hard time believing this was the same woman. "To God be the Glory great things HE hath done," rang out of the congregation in song. A new sense of purpose and of the Lord's presence settled over the folk of this little country church.

Amy, Zain and Natasha's second born, was a gift from God. After Ann, they were unable to have any more children. The Lord placed Amy in their arms through young woman who, many years ago, chose to save a life rather than end an innocent one. Zain and Natasha were introduced to this troubled teen, Karen, at the church where Zain was the assistant pastor. Scared, with this new life growing inside her, she chose adoption and the Lord opened the doors wide. A small, hand-stitched picture was placed over the bed of this wonderful gift and mom and dad lived for it. They have been mom and dad to her from that day and counting. Life is precious and Zain and Natasha could not fathom how an unborn life could ever be treated with so little care.

Now a grown lady, Ann had been through many trials of her own. Just out of high school and ready to take on the world, Ann stood before the church with smiles and dreams, and a new husband, only to be crushed with a life-altering action; divorce. No father wants to see his daughter go through a divorce, yet it happens, and to Zain's heartbreak, twice. Now, with a new husband and baby, mom and dad needed to show their love unconditionally.

It became necessary to add to the family haven once again. Zain chuckled, recalling the first time he took his new son-in-law, Jim, into his confidence about the buried secret that few knew about. Jim told him afterwards that as they were descending the steps to the secret entrance, he wondered if this would be the last time anyone would see him. What a surprise when Zain opened a door that appeared to be ordinary to find a safe-like door and a whole house before him.

The Lord always knows just what is needed and what Jim brought to the family was excellent hunting skills with the bow and arrow. Jim's passion was practiced many times, shooting at targets with a longing for deer season to arrive. This too changed with the great 'meltdown.' Hunting season was now governed by the need to provide, not by the government that was placed in name only. Private property was no longer patrolled by local law enforcement and hunting is a skill that has never gone out of style in this part of America.

Zain recalled his phone conversation with Amy the day before the power failed. "Hi sweetie," he had said, "what is going on with my daughter and grand-baby?" "Oh Daddy," she replied, "I am having a hard time finding enough food to feed my family." Zain said, "I know what you are going through and that is why I called you. I believe we have reached the time when we should be all living together." "But Dad, Jim is at work and will not get paid if he doesn't finish the job," Ann explained. "That may be true," Zain replied, "but I have been watching the news and I am telling you that there is no time to spare and you should come home today." "Wow Dad! If you are saying it like that, I have to believe you are right! I have come to realize that when I don't listen to you I get in bad messes. I want the Lord to bless and He seems to be giving you the wisdom that we need. Tonight, after work, Jim and I and will pack up your granddaughter and the truck and make our way home. We should be there sometime after dinner." When Zain told Natasha, she sighed, "OK now I can rest."

Their arrival was like a family reunion. Mom cried tears of relief to have her family safe. Zain thought perhaps he should not have sounded so urgent, but he was seeing things developing that caused the hair on the back of his neck to stand up. The news was reporting what they were calling, rolling blackouts. These were being purposefully caused to prevent total collapse of an over-tasked wiring system that should have been replaced ages ago. The investors were not willing to put money into a pit that produced no profit.

Getting the three settled in their new home was easy. Amy was here helping every day and knew the layout and the sleeping assignments. Her family would occupy the first room to the left of the entrance. Familiarity with the layout was important because the emergency escapes were between each room. They were practiced each time the family visited the subterranean home so that the exit plan was second nature all.

Zain and Natasha also went down to their new home and settled into their assigned bedroom. It felt surreal back when Zain spoke of a time that they may need such a room but quite another feeling to actually make up the bed and get ready for the unknown. Ann and Dawson joined them with their three children as well. With the young children tucked in for the night, the older children and adults sat in the common area with the television on the news, listening to the serious discontentment developing in the world and the complete lack of promised government control. Zain chose to secure the power to the upper house and activate the security system. Although he believed this action to be premature, it was good to get into such a habit.

Once the doors were closed, he was convinced that all would have a good night sleep.

What came on the news the next morning confirmed what Zain saw coming. The news reporters said that they were not sure how much longer there would be broadcasts, as they also needed to be with their families in this time of turmoil. Reports were rolling in from the previous night that widespread riots were occurring, not only in America, but globally. Distrust of governments had crossed all borders and families living in countries with little tillable land, or means of supplying the people with food, were calling for peace and order so that they could assist in food distribution. That was the official report, but the cable news stations were reporting that food was in dangerously low supply with little to no relief in sight. Some government officials were already calculating the impact on lives although they were reluctant to predict the number of deaths that would occur without some kind of major relief.

Where is God? Zain knew all this was the result of decades of rejecting the Lord and His mercy. News reports said that there could be millions, perhaps billions, of lives that would be lost. Zain believed this to be a conservative estimate because no 'reasonable' newscast was willing to state that the world was in such trouble, but he knew it was. For political parties to actually ask all God-fearing men and women to pray to whatever god they believe in was another blatant example that the "Lord of Lords' had still not been acknowledged. So where is God? He is still where

He always was; on His throne in heaven, while the world refuses to call on the only hope they have.

The family gathered around the breakfast table and began to implement the security protocol that had been written down many months prior to, and for, this situation. The men would be in charge of the security of the family, which included the house and grounds, including the gardens. As time progressed other duties would be added. Duties like fishing and hunting for supplemental food and fresh meat for the table as well as canning and preserving for lean times. There was no need for further discussion as each family member knew the seriousness of the situation and while they were praying that the Lord would come quickly, they were prepared to wait and watch passionately. The house upstairs would be inspected each morning and the security system would be disconnected so that it would appear as a normal, large family home, insuring that the underground home would remain secret and intact. Though they had all the electricity necessary to run several households, they hung their clothes out on the line like the others living around them. This attention to detail would keep them from attracting any attention and the Roberts family would appear to be struggling to survive like the rest of the world. Canned goods and the non-perishable meals that were in storage would be kept out of sight. Being in the vicinity of farms, it would not look suspicious to have animal hides curing and fresh meat would be appreciated. Officially, they owned 30 acres of land but there was an additional 1000 acres of government land that was seldom visited and never hunted by anyone but this family. This would be of great use should the government fail and the Lord tarry.

# MELTDOWN

# Chapter 7

# Family

What is family? By simple definition it would be the relationship one has with members that have been born into immediate blood relations. Zain believed he had redefined that in many ways. A family can be a close group of people with a similar interest or goals. Church members, for two millennial, have referred to each other as brother and sister because of what Christ had done for them. Family, in the Roberts home, is considered to be anyone that comes to visit more than once. Immediate family is made up of people who know you and still decide to like you. That was Zain's position when he allowed others to join his immediate family. He smiled to himself as he reminisced about his family and about Kairi in particular.

She came to the Roberts family as a scared, young lady with nowhere else to go. Natasha and Zain offered her a bed, hot meals and called her granddaughter. People change and with Kairi this proved to be the case. As days turned into weeks, and weeks into months, there had been a transformation that everyone in the family had hoped for. Often, with an older child in this situation, they are set in their ways, making the possibility of significant change unlikely, but Christ can change a heart and with that comes a changed life. Her first comment that gave Zain great hope came after dinner just a few weeks after she came to live with them, and long before the Meltdown. They were all laughing at a family memory shared when Kairi said, "Paw-Paw, we never sat around the dinner table and laughed like you do. We would just go to the stove, grab what was cooked, and go back to our own bedrooms to eat. I think I like this better." Zain tried to explain to her that this is what holds a family together and told her she was welcome to laugh with them at every dinner. From that day forward, Kairi didn't seem to mind when it was her turn do chores around the house. Feeling like a family member, it was just what you do.

Lately, there was a new love in Kairi's life; the art of bow hunting. Add to that a strong desire to learn medicine, with an emphasis on midwifery for home childbirth and you could see God directing her for a special purpose. One day while Jim was shooting his bow, Kairi came over to watch. She began to ask questions and it wasn't long before there was a bow in her hand as well. Learning to shoot is pretty simple but proficiency is learned through practice and experience. Jim provided Kairi with her first lessons in aiming and shooting safety.

After that, not a day went by that she did not take time to shoot. To better acquaint her with proper technique, she was not given sights. Jim instructed her, saying, "Kairi, point the arrow like it's your finger and then release the string and the arrow will go where you pointed." As the days passed the distance she practiced increased. Her fingers were worn numb but she did not give up. Jim taught her some exercises to strengthen her shoulders and arms and within a few weeks the results were noticeable, with definition of muscle mass building. This was beneficial for more than shooting; it helped Kairi with the numerous other activities she was now doing as part of the Roberts family. Each day her shooting became more controlled until she could be sixty feet from her target and was placing her arrows in a pattern of her choosing. Imagine Zain's surprise when she could draw a smiley face at sixty feet, complete with a nose in the bull's-eye as her final shot. Next came three-dimensional targets. This was important so Kairi could transition from shooting at targets to shooting at live animals for food. With a steady hand she took aim at her first target only to miss. One genuine trait Kairi possessed was patience. It did not take more than a few shots for her adjust to the new target and soon her aim was deadly. In the woods, one chance is usually all that is given before the animal scampers to safety, so that summer, practice took up much of her free time. When fall arrived, Jim took Kairi into the woods but it took a bit of persuading to get Kairi comfortable with the idea that what she would shoot is what we would eat and that meat comes from living creatures that give their life so we can live. Squirrel was on the plates for dinner that night, with plenty of family bonding and fun. Plans were laid for rabbit season and then deer season.

In addition to Kairi mastering the bow, Zain also spent time with the entire family, going over some simple defensive moves that could be beneficial if a weapon were not available. They spent several weeks practicing moves so the body would react rather than panic. Little did anyone realize how valuable this training would be for Kairi and Temperance.

In the spring of their senior year of high school they were at school enjoying their last days at the school where they spent the last four years. While walking through the halls reminiscing, a man stepped out from nowhere and grabbed Temp's hand. Without thinking, she stepped toward the predator throwing him off balance. At the same time that he stepped back to get control of his prey, Temperance fell backwards and let her right leg fly with a force that she was not ready for! Adrenaline had kicked in and the left knee of the predator gave way and bent in a direction that was not natural. At first no one saw the knife in his other hand but when she saw it, Kairi kicked the knife out of his and stepped on the throat of the now, laid out predator. She pulled out the knife that she secretly carried and held it to his throat while dialing 911. When the police arrived the predator's knife was retrieved for fingerprints and Kairi surrendered her personal protection so the police could log it in as evidence. It was a wonder that the surveillance cameras were up and running and, by the next school day, Temperance and Kairi were heroes. There was an attempt to cite Kairi with possession of a concealed weapon but it fell on deaf ears as the media replayed the brave action of these two well-trained and confident teens over and over again. Shortly after that event, Kairi and Temperance headed off to college. Temp, with a love with culinary arts, wanted to become a famous chef while Kairi had not wavered with her resolve to help bring new life into this world.

Another surprise to Kairi was the attention she received while shooting her bow in the archery area at school. One of the members of the archery team sat and videotaped her as she easily moved into other shooting positions and found the bull's-eye each and every time. The coach was shown the video of this noteworthy shooting and Kairi immediately was offered a full ride scholarship if she would join the team and help with training this fledgling team. She became the anchor of the team and they rose to national champions. When Olympics were spoken about, Kairi declined the offer and entered into her internship for midwives.

When she came back home after completing her training, Temperance had already started a very successful restaurant. It had a reputation for great meals and desserts that had been written about in numerous magazines as well as awards being won for many of them. As time passed, the girls came home often and helped during the construction phase of the family house. They also spent much time personalizing their assigned rooms in the safe house. There was always plenty of time to shoot or take a stroll in the woods. With a great fear of darkness, it was a long time before Kairi could comfortably walk through the woods without any light available. Little did she know how important that skill would be to her. The two young women spent all the time they could together in the woods. Temperance was a modern-day trick shooter with her .22 caliber rifle and Kairi spent much of her waking time with a bow in her hand. Night and day apart, their friendship remained unwavering. Zain enjoyed the memories that he shared with his family members and thanked God often for family.

Snapping himself back to reality and knowing it was time to get ready for family Bible time, Zain busied himself with the subject they would study that night. Family devotions were a necessity in this house. Many times a free-for-all erupted when the subject of the Lord's return was the topic. It wasn't a bad thing! The Roberts family watched the news daily and many times it seemed as if the end could not be long. When they saw the news like that, they questioned as to the need for a safe house or food storage if the Lord was returning soon. Zain would smile and say, "If God takes us home then someone else can have this place, but if He tarries and we need it, we will rejoice in this little planning." It seemed like the heavy discussion was really a deep longing for the Lord to return. Their devotions often came with practical applications for getting along with others. This was necessary when time was spent in close quarters, underground.

With the evening meal finished and devotions complete it was time for the family to settle in for a night of rest. Each person had his own duties and soon the underground safe house was properly secured with monitors and alarms set. Retiring for the night, Zain thought to himself, "Surely this is what God intended when he spoke about family."

# MELTDOWN

# Unintended Consequences

# Chapter 8

What President Jesse James and his co-laborers around the world did not understand were the unintended consequences of their actions. The people who received the benefit of this financial "reset" would cheer and champion the plan but those that did not receive any benefits would grumble, complain, and ultimately do what they could to try to stop this from happening. What was the end result? Power companies were not paid by customers. The government took control over the power companies but the workers refused to work even though they were promised their pay would be restored and all that back pay would be paid, but without a paycheck the incentive to work became less and less. The domino effect continued and it did not take long for the electric grid to fail, in turn causing the natural gas and propane services to be suspended which then caused fuel to be delivered less effectively. There were long lines of vehicles waiting to fill up and as supply dwindled and demand rose, prices began to skyrocket. With no power, the banking industry was unable to keep up with transactions and the fall began.

President James sat with his advisers reviewing the catastrophic events of the day before. They were all in disbelief! They had not foreseen any downside to their actions and, as much as it was promoted, it appeared that they could not stop the natural tendency of man toward greed and self-preservation. It was clear that they were not moving in the direction that was intended. The intention was that the world would rejoice over this financial freedom and no country would be considered greater than another. The least affected were those countries that had no consistent power grid or infrastructure to begin with. For them, it was business as usual. For countries that had been accustomed to having everything at their fingertips for many years, like America, this was a new learning curve. So, in a sense, President James received exactly what he intended; all men would be equal on this earth and no country would be better than another. Of course he thought that the rest of the world would rise to the status of America but, instead, America fell to the status of the rest of the world.

The Secretary of Homeland Security was speaking to the Secretary of the Interior when they turned to the president to give him more news that he had not anticipated. "Mr. President, we have updated news that food deliveries have fallen short once again and there is now widespread panic in the major cities of America. It seems that the supplies of food in this country are being hoarded by the producers." As the president sat digesting the information that he was given, he had to ask, "Do we know who is holding up the movement of food?" The reply was, "That is why we're here this morning. We must tell you that we suspect the hoarding is being promoted by the Christians. We have discovered that this is due to the fact that eighty-seven percent of all farmers in this country have a firm belief in the antiquated Bible which they say tells them they should take care of their family first before reaching out to others." President James' face was contorted into an ugly caricature of anger, a face that only his closest friends had ever seen. As a politician in the public eye, he would not allow himself to show anger in public. His advisory team had seen it often and knew that he was on the verge of a personal meltdown due to his hatred of the Bible and its believers around this country. After sitting quietly for over five minutes, formulating his words carefully, he spoke, addressing no one in particular on his advisory team. "I want someone to contact our friends in Congress and tell them that we need to draft and pass a bill immediately that will make it illegal for any persons to hold back any vital food to those that live in the city. I want it to include a provision that no family is to have more than a 10-day supply of food on their premises. If more is found, there will be a seizure of said goods, properties, and imprisonment of any member complicit in this act of war against our country." The cabinet meeting turned into a lighter and more festive assembly as it began to formulate how they would take over and run all the farmlands across America. Several phone calls were made that day and without delay several new bills were presented to the Congress and the Senate. After only two days, the bills were signed into law and were sitting on President Jesse James' desk. He called a press conference to 'unleash' this new law publicly and inform the people the law would be implemented effective immediately. While introduction of legislation is a common daily occurrence, once a bill is introduced from Congress to the Senate there are normally conflicts within the bill requiring a joint committee meeting to work out such differences. No one in America seemed to notice the wording in the introduced bills from Congress and the Senate bill was letter perfect and needed no joining of the two bills together, which had not occurred in recent history in America. This was, without a doubt, a backroom deal that was concocted to meet the need of the hour of crisis in America and should it be challenged, anyone opposed would be crushed by the courts of public opinion.

••••••••••••••••••••••••••••••••••••••••••••••••••••••••

Ann, who had never been fond of watching the news or keeping up with the events around the world, soon became interested in the daily news and events that were unfolding. Dawson, Ann's husband, was outside with the kids when Ann heard the TV in the background announce that there would be a special news conference with the President prior to signing a new "Hunger Bill" into effect. The announcer concluded that those in rural farming communities across America should tune in for this monumental briefing. Word had been leaked that enforcement of this new law would be effective immediately and would affect the farmlands across America. Ann stopped what she was doing, went outside, and asked Dawson, "Where is Dad?" "I'm not real sure," he said, "I do believe that I saw him about an hour ago heading over to the generator room for an inspection. I will go and see if I can find him for you. But why? What's up?" "Just tell him that the president is going be on TV signing another bill that will affect the middle of America and that I believe he needs to come and hear." "On my way," Dawson replied, as he put down the rake he'd been using while working in the garden. He looked briefly to make sure that the twins were behaving themselves and then walked down the stairs that would lead to the utility room and the generator. Finding Zain, he said with a smirk "Dad, Ann just asked me to find you and tell you that another announcement from our wonderful president is forthcoming." Though he prayed for the government and leaders, Zain understood the distaste that his family had come to develop for the leader of this country and those that would blindly follow him. He was done checking the generator and determined that it was in perfect running order. Very little maintenance needed to be done in order to maintain the household's independence from the power grid. He put away his tools, wiping the dirt and oil from his hands, and headed for the house so that he could hear the announcement from their wonderful president. He chuckled inwardly at the adjective.

The Roberts family gathered in the living room, sipping fresh water, when the TV news made the announcement that the president of the United States was about to join them. The camera panned to President James as he sat with his customary smile of indifference. He was determined to continue to prove that he was the leader of this country; one that, mere weeks prior, would have been called a great country. He looked into the camera, which was also the teleprompter, and read the following announcement. "My fellow citizens of the World, I come today to direct your attention to my solution for the immediate relief of hunger within this country and around the world. It has been reported that there has been food hoarding taking place. Those that have will not share with those that have not. I want to make myself perfectly clear. This will not be tolerated. Anyone found, from this day forward, to have a food supply of greater than ten days provision will be found in violation of this new law. This law will relieve the starvation being faced in our cities. Food will be redistributed first around our country and then we will reach out to the rest of the world. We're counting on each family member to monitor their stores and report any violations that they see within their family. This is the responsibility of all citizens of this world. No individual should have more than another and the hoarding of food will not be tolerated. The consequences of failing to follow this new law will include the immediate arrest of the individual and all parties complicit to this act. Further, all homes and properties belonging to the law breakers will be confiscated and be deeded to the people of this country and managed by the federal government of the United States. There is no minimum or maximum time that will be served for this offense, but it will be based on the amount of food and supplies that have been seized. What

I'm saying is, the greater the supply hoarded, the greater the sentence. This law will be put into effect immediately but I want you to know that the compassion of this government will allow those who have hoarded food a thirty-day grace period to turn in any excess supplies to their local city government. They, in turn, will be directed to contact the federal government who will facilitate the immediate re-distribution to families in our densely populated cities that lack adequate food supplies. This food supply also includes all personal canned and preserved foods, frozen and dried. As the good book reminds us, we are our brother's keeper! It is our responsibility to ensure those around us have the same access to food, not some with more than they need. With the anticipated passing of this bill into law, a federal task force has already been formed and, if necessary, local and federal law enforcement, in conjunction, will perform house-to- house searches so we can relieve the immediate food shortage facing our cities. Thank you for all that you do and as always God bless you and may God bless the people of this World."

The volume of the TV was turned down as each family member began to contemplate what they had just heard. Amy spoke up first and said, "Did anyone catch his opening phrase that we are no longer citizens of America? When did that take place?" Zain stood so he could address the entire family, "If my research is right, this attack was not on farmers, but on Christians. Nearly ninety percent of American farmers are Christians. Make no mistake about it; he is out to diminish and to destroy our Christian faith. What I need for all you ladies to do, without delay, is to take any excess food supplies and move them down into our home below ground. We need to leave just enough food for three to five days' worth of cooking and baking. There will be a lot of questions when the federal government comes on our property. We need to be well prepared when opening the doors, allowing them to look in, so they have no reason for suspicion or provocation to arrest anyone. I want the old shotgun put in my closet with five shells so if they choose to confiscate our firearms that will be the only one sacrificed. Furthermore, we need to make sure that our children fully understand how important it is to not disclose our living arrangements. As far as the world knows, because of hard times, we are sharing this home together. We have mattresses, blankets, and pillows sitting around the house making it appear that we're sleeping in confined quarters. If we have no more than five days of food stored, they should be satisfied. Each of you know your responsibilities and I'm counting on each and every one to do your part so this family will be strong and able to reach out to our church families who may be in need. I don't want any phone calls made but need the men of the house to personally visit every church member to make sure they have adequate supplies and that any excess food is camouflaged and stored properly with no more than three to five days of food visible at any given time. If we work together, I believe with God's help, we will survive this attack as we have others in the past."

With all that said, each family member busied themselves working, not just as a family but as a team, going through each room collecting unnecessary items and ensuring the instructions given to them were followed. Mothers sat down with their children and reviewed what to say when questioned so that they would not reveal the underground home and the food supplies that each family member knew they had. By the end of the day Zain was satisfied that they complied openly with the new law and that they would not be caught off guard when the inevitable inspection would come from their "wonderful" government.

The following morning an unknown car, occupied by two men, pulled up the driveway and stopped alongside Zain's old truck parked there. "Mr. Roberts," one said, "We are here today to talk to you in our capacity as government leaders to the leader of a community organization. We know that, as a pastor, you have great influence on those who attend your church. We are not here to tell you that you cannot attend church but to ask you to cooperate and convince the families of your church to surrender any food they may have in excess of ten days personal supply so that it can be redistributed to those that have not. Do you understand what we're asking?" Zain, having met the car in the driveway, stood and listened to their "offer." He said, "Let me get this straight. We are not allowed to have food for more than ten days supply. Is that correct?" One of the men, who appeared to be the leader, looked irritated and said, "Did you not hear the news yesterday of the new bill signed into law, effective immediately, that hoarding would not be tolerated in America or around the world any longer?" Zain stood there without displaying any emotion, face-to-face with these government officials. "Yes, I heard the news yesterday and you're welcome to inspect our house and supplies. We are a simple family and have no more than five to seven days of food; we struggle just like everyone else these days. You are welcome to verify that and I will, of course, counsel anyone who asks me to co-operate with law enforcement." "We were hoping you would say that and we would like to take a tour of your house. It is such a beautiful house. It looks new. How old is it?" the quiet man asked. Zain replied, "Only a couple years old. We have been blessed of God and He supplied the provisions for us to build this house. And now, as a wonderful coincidence, it happens to be large enough so that when the recent hardships hit this country, I had enough room to invite my family to come and stay with us."

The government officials walked quietly throughout the house, including each bedroom, and made note that there was a shotgun with five shells which Zain explained was for self-protection against wild animals that might be in the woods. Zain took them downstairs to show them the empty shelves and patiently explained that the harvest had not yet begun, nor the canning season, but he would be glad to share with those in need when the canning season had come to an end. They inquired of him what was in the back room so Zain opened up the storm shelter acting quite pleased that he had space sufficient for his family in case of inclement weather. Satisfied that the house was in compliance, they walked out to inspect the garage and the barn and found no extra food or contraband to report. There was a fifty-pound bag sitting in the corner and though they were not farmers they recognized it as seed and asked, "What is this seed? Could it be used for food?" Zain smiled and said, "Sure if you don't mind eating grass seed! See the field out there that has not yet been harvested? It is my intent to allow the field to rest next year and plant grass so that the cattle will have a place to graze, alleviating the need to feed them throughout the summer." The men looked at each other, satisfied that they were in compliance and turned to the pastor and said, "Thank you for the tour, you have a lovely house. We noticed that you have a shotgun and you mentioned that that was going to be for self-defense, is that right?" "Yes," was all that Zain replied. "Well, I believe we have concluded our inspection and we are satisfied that you are in compliance with the new law. We hope that you will help us out by counseling your parishioners in the necessity of being in compliance." Zain tried not to sound sarcastic as he said, "I will be happy to tell them that I was visited by the government and what your intentions are toward the children of God." These men understood exactly what pastor Zain had said and made an attempted defense of the new law, reminding the pastor that this was not a law against Christians; this was a law to assist the Christians in being compliant with the commands of the Bible. They said, "Good day to you sir," got into their car and quietly turned around and left the property.

Zain knew that this would be the first of many visits and that they must stay vigilant and be ready for inspection with little or no notice and appear to be compliant with the new law and give them no reason to destroy their families. He was also careful in answering their questions. He did not want to lie to them and, if necessary, would ask other questions, diverting their question with a question, praying that they would not pursue it further and ask a question that would cause him to lie. If necessary, Zain would spend time in jail to protect his family and he prayed that God would continue to guard his family and protect them as He had in the past. Zain's personal morals required him to be polite and courteous to visitors. Even those who question who he is and what his intentions are, regardless of his personal desire to stand against this evil. He would stand but he knew that it was only through the power of a Holy God that victory was possible.

• • • • • • • • • • • • • • • • • • • • • • • • • • • • • • • • • • • • • • • • • • • • • • • • • • • • • • • •

Over the next few days the President was pleased with himself as reports began to roll in. The inspections had located scores upon scores of hoarded food supplies. The news reported that trucks were being hired, or forced into service, to distribute the food to the largest of the cities in hopes of curtailing the violence that had plagued them. What President James failed understand was that it was not hunger, but greed, that fed and fueled the angry crowds and that no amount of food would satisfy their hunger. Another unintended consequence, right from the history books; the greed of man's heart could never be satisfied. The president turned his chair around in the Oval Office, leaned back and looked out through the window and asked himself, "What next?"

. . . . . . . . . . . . . . . . . . . . . . . . . . . . . . . . . . . . . . . . . . . . . . . . . . . .

Evening arrived and Zain looked out into the night. He could not see any streetlights illuminated. This night, like any other, the family would quietly retire to their underground home where dinner, family fun, and a time of Bible reading and prayer were waiting. "Heavenly Father, we thank you for another day of protection. We thank you for your provisions and protections of this day. We thank you for the health that you have given to this family. We also pray for our government and this nation. Lord, we see your hand upon us and upon this nation, upon our president and upon our lawgivers, and though we may not understand, we thank you and give praise to you for all these things. We ask that you watch over all the families of this church for the night, granting them a sound night's sleep, that they would rise rested, fulfilled, and ready to serve you. Please, Lord, blind again the eyes of the evil one and open the eyes that are hungry for your Word. This we ask in Jesus name, Amen." As had become the custom, each family stood, exchanged hugs, and soon the family was in the nightly routine making ready for a good night's rest. The security cameras were turned on, the alarms were activated, and Zain was confident that his family was safe and ready to meet another day should God tarry.

# MELTDOWN

## Chapter 9

## Bad News Again

As President Jesse James' cabinet gathered for their morning meeting, a heated discussion broke out about who to allocate the blame to for the economic downfall facing this nation. The brainstorming began with the Secretary of Defense purposing to blame foreign countries who failed to fully understand the economic necessity of the "reset" program. His proposal was simple; that America should wage war on those that did not fully support its policies. A small roar of grumbling came from around the room as each member began to bring forth their own ideas and possible solutions. One by one, each idea was discussed and quickly dismissed. Then the Secretary of Homeland Security quietly proposed what was quickly and unanimously accepted as the master plan. It included not only who they could blame for the downfall of this country but also how they could destroy the Christian religious society once and for all at the same time.

From the ashes of this plan they would be free to create their own ideology, creating a philosophy of what to worship, who to worship, and how to worship. With all in agreement, 'O fateful day,' this country would no longer be a Christian nation. A law would be drafted, a decree would be made, and in a few short weeks this country would no longer celebrate any religious holiday or tolerate any religious assembly. The President thought to himself, "What a masterful plan!" When it was implemented, he would be rid of this religion called Christianity once and for all. He thought the task would be relatively easy because he had the support of both the Senate and the Congress and any opposition that may come would be too little, too late.

That afternoon, in an unscheduled meeting with the majority leader of the Senate and the majority leader of Congress, all three sat in the President's office. He revealed to them the plan that would, once and for all, rid this country of the biased, religious hate that Christians spread around the country. They verbally patted each other on the back, firmly believing that they had made a choice that would put their power base in a permanent and unwavering status. As the President dismissed the two leaders from his office, he encouraged them to quickly draft the law that would solve all of their problems and stop the opposition from this so-called Christian nation.

Bright and early the next morning, both the Senate and the House of Representatives sat down with their team of representatives and wrote the bill that would be named "Freedom from Religion." With little opposition, and even less public knowledge, the bill quickly became law. It was determined that enforcement of this law would begin within 30 days, without any discrimination regarding the size of a congregation. Of course, they believed that if they stopped the largest of churches that the smaller churches would fall one by one.

• • • • • • • • • • • • • • • • • • • • • • • • • • • • • • • • • • • • • • • • • •

There was a hush in the air as the news spread around the world that the current downfall of America was the fault of the Christians, who would not succumb to the demands of the government. In order to expediently repair the government and its financial disarray, it was ordered that no assembly, comprised of a group of more than seven people, was allowed. The only exclusion to this law was directly related family members. Outside of family, there could be no large gatherings without the approval of the benevolent government. This included public demonstrations which the Government hoped would end those taking place in front of the White House and Congress by groups protesting against abortion and reminding lawmakers of their duties to the American people.

True believers knew that this day would come, so it was no surprise to them when the law was signed on a Friday, at five o'clock, with little media coverage. As Christians around the country gathered together, they knew it was only a matter of time before the government would do as they threatened. Arrests would be made! But how could the government arrest a large segment of the population? The answer was right there before them. They would not arrest the general population of people, but rather the leaders, setting an example and placing fear into the hearts of those that remained behind.

With this promised threat in the air, it might be thought on the Sunday morning after the law was enacted that church houses would be empty. Quite the opposite occurred! They were filled to capacity. Even people who had no prior belief in God came looking for hope. The preaching of the Word of God that Sunday morning became an inspiration for many. News reporters stood in disbelief as the reports came in. Thousands of full and over capacity attendance records were reported in churches across the country. What was intended to be a victory against God became a dismal failure. The gospel message is powerful and even more so when the harsh realities of this life settle in. Sin is part of this life and it was necessary for there to be some conviction of it. Not just to bow one's head and to repeat a prayer, but that all who would understand their lost and sinful state and come to know Jesus as Saviour would come with a humble heart and true repentance.

When the little country church Zain pastored met that fateful morning, it was, like so many others, filled beyond capacity. Zain stood behind the pulpit fully ready for the police to bust the doors down and declare this assembly an illegal activity. Hymns were sung, hands were shaken, and the humble preacher of a little country church stood and faithfully proclaimed the Word of God. After the masses had left and the main body of the church remained, the faithful followers gathered together around their pastor, a humble servant of God, and lifted him in up prayer, praying together and asking God for protection, guidance, and most of all, His will.

Lights out for the Roberts family came at the normal time, but as husband and wife lay together, a quiet peace overshadowed their lives. Though turmoil was all around them, Zain and his wife, Natasha, could rest in the knowledge that God was in control. Whatever happened, it was the will of God and therefore was not theirs to manipulate, but accept. *"Great peace have they which love thy law and nothing shall offend them"* was a verse that they had claimed many times, but that night it was so very real to each of them, as real as the two arms in which they fell fast asleep, knowing that God was in control.

●●●●●●●●●●●●●●●●●●●●●●●●●●●●●●●●●●●●●●●●●●●●●●●●●●●●●●●●

President James called an emergency cabinet meeting early that evening to formulate a plan to address the catastrophe of the day. It was clear that the people of this nation were not going to obey this new law and that enforcement was impossible. Once again the members were in disarray. The trusted advisors could not agree as to the best plan of action. The President was clearly irritated when a staff member stepped in to hand him a repulsively familiar cell phone. Jesse had assumed that he was the President, and a power in this plan, but it was becoming clear that he was a mere pawn to a man that very few people knew was involved in the reformation of this world. "Good evening," President James answered the phone, believing it to be the person simply referred to as the "secretary." He was completely unprepared for the voice on the other end. By the voice that replied, he knew he was speaking with Donald Maddox, his secret benefactor and the real source of power, not just in America but the world over. "It seems we have underestimated the resolve of church attending people," Donald Maddox said, "but retracting the law would perhaps be a hasty decision. Instead, I would like you to announce a retraction but allow the law to remain in the background should the need of it arise in the future." "That is a great plan," replied the puppet president as the phone in his hand went dead.

"This is our new plan," the president said, after regaining his composure and putting on his Presidential persona. "We will announce the retraction of the "Freedom from Religion Act" but will not actually remove it from the law books. It will remain on the books in the event we have need of it in the future. We have underestimated the spirit and resolve of the Christians around this land but, mark my words, they will not have the last word on this matter."

The meeting was over and each member knew it was time to make ready for a very busy day on Monday. After the public announcement, with no mention of the under the table deal, they expected a lot of public response. Of course, since they controlled the media, they knew the press would remain silent on the matter, keeping the public appeased while the law secretly remained on the books.

•••••••••••••••••••••••••••••••••••••••••••••••••

Monday, Zain and his family rose for their daily chores and after breakfast was finished the news was tuned in on the radio. The new anchor was saying, "We have just witnessed the repeal of the "Freedom from Religion Act." If our research is correct, this would be the fastest any bill was signed into law and then repealed. Again, let me say, we have just witnessed the repeal of the "Freedom from Religion Act." The explanation handed down by a press release from the Press Secretary of the White House stated that it was an impractical law and was poorly implemented. The blame for the inability to enforce the law was placed on the local law enforcement community and they reported that no future statement would come from the President.

Ann and Amy looked at each other and a high five was exchanged as they turned to spread the good news. Neither wanted to see their dad taken from the church in handcuffs and it appeared that the Lord had yet again protected not only this church, but all the churches around America. Zain and Natasha walked into the room where the family had been listening to the radio and wondered what all the commotion was for. "We won!" both girls said simultaneously. "The 'Freedom from Religion Law' was just repealed."

Zain and Natasha looked at each other and, without realizing the work that was taking place in their hearts, the Holy Spirit revealed to both of them that this was a lie being perpetrated by the press corp. Zain spoke, saying, "I believe this is an attempt to deceive people into believing this law was repealed. We have not seen the last attempt by our government to destroy the work of God. We will rejoice yet remain vigilant. We will watch what they will do next." The girls agreed that their dad was right but they chose to remain optimistic. "Well enough of the news we can't trust! We need to be busy telling people the news we can trust," Zain said, as he turned the radio.

He had been expecting to hear news of many arrests and persecutions only to hear wonderful news. The government had been so overwhelmed by the response of the American people that the law was retracted and pastors would not be in violation for preaching the Word of God. The family joined in prayer, thanking God for the safety He once again provided to their family.

Subsequently, a discussion was made at the church house of who would stand up and take the place of the pastor should this law be re-enacted, and the pastor be taken into custody. It was decided that no family member had a claim to any throne. The throne a pastor represents is not the throne of a father or a husband, it is a throne of an Almighty God. God would direct who would lead His flock should the pastor be taken. All the men of the church agreed that they would stand and take the place of their pastor, even if it meant being arrested and joining him in jail.

Over the next several days Pastor Zain encouraged the church families to remain optimistic but ever watchful. The government had again proven to be unreliable. Timely announcements were made at church on Sunday about the repeal of the "Freedom from Religion" law and the church agreed to keep this matter in prayer as they continued to serve.

The text that Sunday morning came from the Book of Nehemiah and pastor Zain expounded from the Bible that there was a necessity to build and yet remain watchful, weapons in one hand and tools in the other, standing guard when necessary so the work could go on. A season of prayer followed the morning service and most stayed for prayer as well as to catch up on all the news around town. Zain leaned against the church house and thought to himself, "It must have been like this in the early days of our country. The church is the center of our lives and we meet together not just to hear the preaching of God's Word but for fellowship and to encourage each other. WOW! What a great God we serve."

# Meltdown

## The Shepherd

## Chapter 10

The Roberts family had developed an early to bed, early to rise, schedule. Living on a farm is rewarding but it is also physically tasking. With no windows in the underground house, alarm clocks were set for 5:00 AM. Zain listened as he heard the other family members began to stir for the morning chores with breakfast to follow. Each family member worked on their assigned morning chores, anticipating a breakfast that included fresh eggs that had been gathered along with fresh bread baked the day before. With their chores completed, the family gathered around the table in the aboveground house for breakfast. Jim looked up from his plate when he thought he saw movement out of the corner of his eye. Sure enough, a bike was coming up the driveway and the rider, a teenage boy, looked like he was on a mission. Zain excused himself and went out to greet the young visitor. He was a member of the church from a large family and he wasted no time riding up to Pastor Zain with a message from his father.

"Pastor," the young teenager said, "the phones are not working again so my dad asked me to ride over here and see if you could come to the house for a few moments. He said it's very important." He gave no other information but there was clearly urgency in the young teenager's voice. Pastor Zain instructed the young man to place his bike in the back of the pickup and told him that he would be just a moment. He went back into the house and relayed the information to his wife, Natasha, and told her that he would be back as soon as possible. He turned to his family and asked them to pray for the unknown circumstances and that God would give him wisdom for whatever was before them. He quietly turned, keys in hand, jumped into his truck and headed out to help with what, he did not know.

As Pastor Zain pulled into the boy's driveway, it was clear that something was out of place. He quietly prayed that the Lord would give him wisdom to help in any way possible. Sitting on the steps leading up to the porch was Jim Wright, a faithful member of his country church. Jim's head was in his hands and he was looking down but Zain recognized by the heaving of his shoulders that Jim was weeping. This was not the big, strong Jim that he had come to know and love through many years of service together. This was more like a man who was beaten and without hope.

Not knowing the circumstances that caused Jim to have such grief, Pastor Zain stood quietly, waiting to be told of a catastrophe. After a few moments Jim opened his eyes, realizing that his pastor was there. He looked up with tears running down his face and said, "Pastor, I know you have already gone through something like this but I just don't know what to do." Taking a deep breath, he began to describe that while he was finishing his morning chores he heard one of his daughters scream. He quickly rounded the corner of the barn in the direction the scream had come from and saw a man holding a knife to his daughter's throat! "Pastor, he demanded that I step back and allow him to pass so he could simply take my daughter and the food that he had gathered and they would be on their way," Jim exclaimed. "There was no way I was going to let that happen. As soon as the man was not looking, I drew the pistol that I carry behind my back." Once again, Jim began to weep, as reality set in. He had taken the life of a man in order to save the life of his daughter. "Pastor, I killed a man. I know you spoke of this before and I agreed that you had done the right thing, but it's different when it is you that squeezed that trigger! How do I get past this?"

Pastor Zain turned toward the front door where Mrs. Wright and her daughter were standing. He said, "Sister Wright, how is she doing?" "Thank the Lord, she is physically unharmed," she answered, "but at this very moment, she is standing here beside me covered with blood that is not hers and we don't know what to do! Do we contact the police so they can gather evidence and possibly separate our family, or do we do nothing?" Zain had dealt with similar circumstances before so his instructions came from personal experience, not from guessing what the law would or would not do. "Do you have a digital camera?" he asked. Mrs. Wright turned and walked into the house and came back with a camera. "Great," Zain said. "The next thing that we need to do is take some pictures of your daughter and the bloodstained clothes. Then we need to take pictures of the perpetrator and his weapon and keep them for future reference and evidence. Since the phones are out and the police have already instructed me in the handling of events such as these, we will deal with this in a humane and proper manner. We will not involve the police at this time, as they are unable to handle any emergencies in this rural area in a timely manner."

After the pictures were taken, the sons of the family went out to the edge of their property and began the task of digging a grave for this unknown man. Jim and Zain loaded the body on a trailer hooked to the tractor and headed out to the man's final resting place. The man had no identification papers or unusual marks on him so an unmarked grave for an unknown man was his final resting place. The family gathered at the graveside to give thanks unto God for the safety of this family. Zain led them in a prayer and asked God to give peace in the midst of the storm.

Pastor Zain insured Jim that he had done the right thing protecting his family. He explained to Jim that taking a life in defense of his family was not breaking God's commandment, "Thou shalt not kill." He told Jim that this commandment was one of instruction that a man should commit no murder upon another individual. He told Jim that self-defense and murder were two different actions. The words seemed hollow, even though they were true, and the pastor knew it. Deep down Zain was still struggling with the same act that he had committed, but he knew he must give sound, biblical counsel and encouragement to this dear friend. He also shared a truth with Jim that had privately brought some peace in his own life. "Jim," said Zain, "the police reviewed my case and their reply to me was simple. If you're a man who can kill and feel no remorse, then you are a dangerous man. No man should be comfortable taking a life, innocent or not." Before leaving, Pastor Zain once again gathered the family and prayed. While he was praying, surprisingly, the phone began to ring. Mrs. Wright quietly stepped into the house to answer the phone. When the prayer was ended she called out the door to the pastor and said, "Your wife is on the phone." Zain walked into the house and was told of another emergency call from another family of his church. Pastor Zain said, "Well, the phones are working again," and excused himself. He jumped into his truck and headed out to help with the new emergency.

By the end of the day the pastor had been called to four homes and graciously had been fed by one family, although they too had to deal with a similar tragedy. He walked into his house just as his family was sitting down for the evening meal. Dawson was the first to speak saying, "Dad, you look like you have been in a battle today." Zain thought to himself without saying it aloud, "Son, you have no idea what it's like to be a pastor." He smiled at his family, changed the subject, and asked how all of their day had gone. He had surrendered to be a pastor, not his children nor his grandchildren. They need not be privy to all the details of his daily routine as he tended to his flock. At that thought, a familiar feeling from the Holy Spirit reminded him that the church where he served was in fact not "his flock." Zain was reminded that King David of old was a shepherd, yet the Bible said that he was a shepherd of his father's flock. Zain quietly acknowledged his error and asked the Lord to forgive him for speaking incorrectly of God's church.

Sunday came and once again the church house was filled to capacity. His text that morning was from Psalm 23. He spent a brief moment explaining why David was a shepherd and that being a shepherd included truth without compromise and showing God's love without end. He spent time, verse by verse, expounding on the Word of God. Nearing the end of the service, Pastor Zain, once again, shared the message of the Gospel. It was the greatest news of all time to those that are lost and come to realize their need of a Saviour. Pastor Zain closed the service with prayer and yet, without any unusual prompting, he found several people gathering at the front of the church, kneeling and asking Jesus to be their Saviour. Zain stood in awe, giving thanks to the Lord for saving souls and adding to His kingdom. One by one they came to the pastor to announce that they had found forgiveness in Jesus Christ and they wanted to follow in believers' baptism. Very few people had left the church service, so Pastor Zain turned to the families and announced the new brothers and sisters in Christ. Applause followed and a time of rejoicing caused the church doors to remain open for an extra hour before they went home for the day.

The following week the baptismal was filled. One by one each new believer entered the water to be immersed. Prior to their baptism, each one gave a short testimony of their new-found life in Christ and their desire to make this public statement, without being ashamed of what Christ had done for them. Zain reminded them, as they gladly received the gift of salvation and were baptized, that they were added to the church membership. Fellowship came easy on days like these and good news was a welcome excuse for spending time together. With food currently being carefully accounted for, having a "potluck" meal was big thing. Each family chose from the bounty from their gardens and hunts for the feast that was spread out on the tables in the church house basement. Dinner at church, though rare these days, was considered necessary for families to fellowship and grow in Christ and it was a great opportunity for the new members to share in the bounty of those that had plenty.

The women gathered together and giggles and laughs could be heard from them. The kids headed outside where a game of tag was formed and their running and laughing brought smiles to the parents. The men gathered and exchanged the news of the week and it seemed like life was like it used to be.

As the men gathered together, Zain decided this was a good time share his heating discovery with the men of the church so they could prepare for the cold months ahead. The plans were simple enough and supplies were still available at the local hardware store. He gave each man present an easy to read schematic that included a materials list of what was needed to convert water into energy. After gathering hydrogen that could be stored in the empty propane tanks, the propane furnaces and stoves could be modified to utilize the new fuel source. The men stood speechless as Zain explained his design. He told them that he would come and help any family to convert their cooking stove and furnaces into this free, energy efficient method to keep their families warm for the winter. The men had tears in their eyes as they realized that their family would be warm this winter with a very small investment of time and money. It was agreed that the pastor would help one family, who then, in turn would help another.

Time passed all too quickly and it came time to head for their homes so chores could be accomplished. Harvest and canning season would soon be upon them and fellowship would be limited until winter. Within days, the families of the church were using the new fuel source and they rejoiced, praising for God for his provision.

••••••••••••••••••••••••••••••••••••••••••••••••••••••

On Saturday, President James took an unexpected and unannounced trip to meet with the primary designers of the "Reset." He was instructed to fly in a much smaller plane than the typical 747 of Air Force One. This requirement did not make him happy, as he had grown accustomed to his rather plush accommodations. When the small plane landed and the door was opened, President James saw a line of small, unmarked jets. He realized the reason it was necessary for him to use a smaller jet. No bands played, no fanfare for diplomatic purposes was heard. Then a rather comfortable golf cart pulled up to the bottom of the stairs and a young man invited the president to join him. There was no need to ask any questions, he knew the driver was just that, and only assigned to take him to the designated place for this unannounced meeting.

When Jesse James entered the room he saw a series of tables forming a semicircle with chairs facing toward the front where a podium with a microphone stood. Every chair had a name tag and a headset as well as paper and pens. The host, looking around, spoke into the microphone at the podium, "Ladies and gentlemen, it appears that all are now present and accounted for so if you would please take your seats."

For the next several hours each leader was feverishly taking notes as a new phase of the Reset was unfolded and revealed to them. President James discovered that he would become the new leader over one of ten regions that the world had been divided into, no longer just the president of the United States. His area of responsibility would now include Canada, America, and half of Central America. It was explicitly stated that this information was not to be released until approved and directed by this central committee.

President James leaned back into his seat, realizing that his role as the president of United States would soon come to an end. He was eager for his role as a ruler of one of ten regions of the new world to begin. He felt quite satisfied that he had been recognized as a world leader and was happy to be a contributor to this new world order that would soon be unfolded. With this information presented to them by the elusive Donald Maddox, they were instructed by his secretary that all their planes had been properly refueled and that the crews were all rested and ready for their journey home. During the flight home, President James determined who would be let in on this 'secret of secrets.' It would include his wife Susan, the Secretary of Homeland Security, as well as a few other trusted associates. His personal notes would be placed in a secret safe behind one of the pictures in the oval office that he had installed for the most sensitive, presidential eyes only, information.

After several hours of flight, his unmarked aircraft landed and taxied to the same hangar from which they started, without fanfare. The tow bar was connected to the plane, the hanger opened, and the tractor began the last leg of this monumental journey. So much information contained in the handouts given and personal notes he had taken would not see the light of day until such a time that he was so directed. If Jesse learned anything on this journey, this president, soon to be regional king, learned that if you want real power, you must wait until it is given to you. This kind of power was not passed down from father to son, or mother to son, but could only be conferred upon one by someone greater.

Jesse spent the rest of the evening in the safe room of the White House basement with his wife, Susan, where he was confident that no recording devices had been placed. He showed her the notes and information that had been given to him. Susan responded to the news with delight, realizing that she and her husband were in the right place at the right time, knowing the right people. They would soon find themselves rich beyond belief with indescribable power. Susan thought to herself, "If there were a god, I would certainly take a moment and thank him or her for this wonderful gift!"

After reviewing all the notes, President James placed everything in an unmarked folder and carried it to the oval office and placed them in the secret safe. Closing the safe, Jesse placed his right hand on a pad that verified his fingerprints; the only possible way that the safe could be opened. With this task completed he mumbled under his breath, "Until such a day," as if speaking to the safe and the instructions within.

# MELTDOWN

## Hunting Party

# Chapter 11

The morning started like any other morning; there is no sunrise or sunset when you live underground. The alarm clock went off at 5 o'clock as it did each morning and Zain rolled out of bed to start his morning as usual with a shower, cup of coffee, and reading the Word of God. One by one his family began to stir and life underground resembled what could now be called normal. During breakfast, Zain turned to Kairi and asked her what her plans were for the day. "Well," she replied, "I don't have anything special planned. Is there something that I can do to help?" Zain thought to himself how grateful he was to have such an understanding and helpful granddaughter. "I was listening to the news earlier on the shortwave radio," Zain said, "and the talk is that this emergency food rationing could be extended for several months. I believe it is time that we expanded our hunting so we can be a benefit, not only for our family, but our neighbors as well." Kairi replied, "That's great. How can I help?"

"I was wondering if you and Temperance would like to scout out a new area in the woods and see if you can come up with any fresh meat that can be useful for our community," Zain asked. Kairi and Temperance looked at each other with a gleam in their eyes and both turned to Zane and said in unison, "We would be happy to go and help out Paw-Paw." "Why don't you take the four-wheeler about a mile down the road? There is a bit of woods that I know you are familiar with and could help us out with a fresh hunting area." Zain explained.

The two girls cleared the dishes and excused themselves to make preparations for a day of hunting. Each of them slipped into their camouflage hunting equipment. Kairi grabbed her bow and arrows while Temperance reached into the closet and selected her favorite firearm for the day. Her weapon of choice would be a simple .22 rifle with a scope and sound suppresser along with a 9MM sidearm for personal protection. Just as had been rehearsed, the two girls also put in their pockets what they referred to as the GPS panic button. This was a simple communication device that allowed the family to go off into different areas and yet stay connected to the unit if an emergency arose.

The ride down to the woods was uneventful. They carefully dismounted the vehicle, placed it in an inconspicuous area, and removed the key to prevent anyone else from taking their vehicle. Just as Paw-Paw had suggested, the land had many signs of wild game animals rummaging through this area. As was their custom, Kairi used her bow on large game and Temperance helped out by collecting the little critters that God had created so that man could live. About a quarter mile into the woods the girls heard a sound. It was a familiar sound of men and women talking. Kairi was curious as to who these people might be and whether they were friend or foe. Quietly, the two girls wove their way through the woods, stepping carefully over the twigs so that very little sound was made. Unbeknownst to them, there were lookouts posted behind the trees. Without warning, Temperance and Kairi were surrounded!  Without putting up a fight, they relinquished their weapons to this group that was clearly a desperate band scavenging for food.

A man, who could only be described as the leader of this band, came up to the girls and made a comment that sent shivers down their backs. "I see that you've been all hunting today!" the man said in an overly pleasant voice, "We are surely going to enjoy the meal that you provided for us. From here on out, you two are going to join our band and be part of our family and hunt for us." He continued, asking, "What are your names and how old are you?" Temperance, being the shy one, would not look up and she was determined that she would not answer them no matter the cost. Kairi, who knew Temperance well, became the spokesman for the two. "My name is Kairi and my sister's name is Temperance." Kairi replied. "Sisters? I doubt that," said the leader of the pack. "You two don't look anything alike." Kairi replied tartly "You're absolutely right, we're not biological sisters. We are sisters because we are both part of God's family." "Oh! You are part of that religious group that we've heard about around these parts. No matter, you'll learn to serve our needs no matter what you think. You are now part of our family and we will tell you what to do, and we will tell you when to do it. Is that understood?" the man asked.

Kairi, without batting an eye, looked straight into the eyes of this aggressive man and said, "Sir, I don't know who you are but if you know what's good for you, you'll let me and my sister leave before there's any trouble." Without warning, the man swung his hand and the back of his hand hit Kairi on the cheek. She saw from the corner of her eye the beginning of the swing of his arm and had relaxed her neck so that when he struck her face it was a mere glancing blow instead of the full impact he intended it to be. She twisted her head as if she'd been stricken hard and was careful not to stand defiantly. He did not know that both Kairi and Temperance had, the moment that they realized that there was a problem, touched the panic button in their pockets and they knew help was on the way. Not only was that button a distress signal, it was also a GPS homing signal. The handheld device that it linked with would soon hone in on their location. It also activated a silent radio signal that would be picked up as the rescue team drew closer to the units.

Several hours passed by and instructions were given to the girls regarding how they would be guarded that night and what their daily duties would be. They would not be left unattended or unsupervised until they had proven that they could be trusted to be part of this new family. Both Temperance and Kairi silently accepted the instructions, knowing that this ordeal would soon come to an end. Without hesitation, they joined their temporary "new family" and helped by gathering firewood. They stood by as this 'would be' family took all the fresh meat that they had gathered for the day and began to prepare it for the group's evening meal.

Back at home, about an hour had passed by, when suddenly, an alarm went off. Zain knew something was not right with the girls! He quickly ran over to the control panel and identified that both panic buttons were pushed from his granddaughters, Temperance and Kairi. With both buttons illuminated it was a clear signal that the girls were in grave danger or they would not have pushed them simultaneously. Zain called all the men of the family and they were quickly apprised of the situation. Without a word, they dispersed to neighboring farms to summon help. What seemed like forever but was only a matter of 45 minutes, a band of ten brothers had assembled and were receiving instructions about the alarm that had been set off. As agreed, they quietly moved down to the parcel of land where the radio signal part of the GPS was now tracking the movement of the two young ladies.

With great care the men split up and began to surround the area where the attack had taken place. In the distance, apparently not worrying about sound or interruption, the band of thieves could be heard celebrating as they prepared the meal that they had not earned. The lookouts had been spotted and neutralized so they could not sound the alarm as the rescue party prepared a daring rescue. Each of the 10 men had a headset on and could hear Zain's instructions about the next move. Four of the men were expert sharpshooters and they quietly found a vantage point where they could set up shop and prepare for what they hoped would not be a battle, but be ready to execute the plan to rescue these two dear children.

Zain, giving last minute instructions, told the men that he would make his presence known, giving the marauders a chance to give up the two girls without a fight. He would be counting on the sharpshooters to watch his back and take silent action with the sound suppressed muzzles of their deadly accurate weapons of choice. Quiet mumbles were heard as Zain pushed another button that would vibrate the panic buttons he hoped were still in the possession of Temperance and Kairi. Zain had the advantage of seeing the two girls look at each other and simply nod their head, all the confirmation he needed to know that the buttons were still in their possession and that they were aware of their rescuer's presence. Although Temperance and Kairi had never been in this position before, they had been trained and instructed for such a situation. So they were confident that this ordeal would soon be over.

Zain stood and revealed his position, yet remained silent. One of intruders suddenly did a double take, as if he saw something, but not sure that someone was there. As he zeroed his eyes in, he realized that a man dressed in camouflage was standing there silently with his hands behind his back. The man nudged the guy next to him and pointed and voices rumbled through the band of intruders, who appeared to number around 12 or 14. In short order, the leader was made aware of the presence of the stranger who was intruding on their celebration. He was irritated and short tempered, yet with caution he turned to face Zain and challenged his presence saying, "Mister, I don't know who you are but we are about to celebrate a meal together. If you're here in peace you can come and join us."

Zane stood quietly and did not move. He carefully looked over the group of would-be intruders to ascertain if anyone was alarmed or making any threatening actions toward him. Zain spoke clearly in a normal tone of voice, "I'm here to retrieve my granddaughters and I'm asking you politely to release them and return their hunting utensils and we will be quietly on our way."

The band of intruders began to laugh as if they just heard a joke. Once again the leader said, "Mister, I don't know who you're talking about. These here young ladies are part of our family. They joined with us today and we are prepared to defend them, if necessary." Zain did not attempt to move forward but was very aware that the situation could turn deadly at any moment. He said, "Friend, I don't know who you are and I'm not here for any trouble but I will be taking my granddaughters home today. I'm asking you one more time, release them and hand me the weapons and we will leave peaceably." As Zain expected, one of the men on the outskirts of this group reached for his rifle. In a split second, with nary a hint of the direction from which it came, a shot splintered the handle of the rifle into pieces as a 308 Winchester equipped with a sound suppressor expended another round into this, now useless, piece of metal. Before anyone else had the chance to move toward their weapon,

Zain held out his hand and fired a round into the air from the pistol that he had been holding behind his back. Suddenly, as if someone touched the button as in a game of freeze tag, the group of men froze, not daring to make a move. Zain's voice rang out, "Gentlemen, what you don't know is that you're surrounded. As I told you earlier, we are not here for trouble but to gather up my granddaughters so that they can come and be part of our family once again." "Girls," Zain yelled, "I want you to walk quickly over to your weapons and gather them together. Then I want you to gather each of the firearms from these gentlemen so that we won't have to worry about any future conflict." Without hesitation, Temperance and Kairi dutifully gathered their weapons and the weapons of their "would-be" abductors.

Zane once again spoke up and said, "I asked you peaceably to give up my granddaughters and you refused. That decision is going to cost you your weapons." The leader, now humbled, whined, "Mister, how are we supposed to survive if we have no ability to hunt?" "You should've thought about that when, instead of hunting, you decided to abduct innocent girls and take what they had worked so hard for and attempt to humiliate them into believing that they were to be part of your life. I suggest you that you leave these woods and go back where you came from. If I ever see you here again the outcome will be less appealing than it is right now," Zain informed him

The would-be leader, though clearly humiliated, was also visibly irritated and decided that he would make a last attempt at defiance as

Temperance walked by. He reached behind his back, slipping out a knife and grabbed Temperance around the neck. Once again, a silent round was fired and the hand that was holding the knife would never be the same. Without missing a beat, Temperance reached down and gathered the dropped weapons and fell into place behind Kairi and the two girls made their way toward their rescuer and grandfather.

Zain signaled his team and they all stood up, revealing to the intruders that they were indeed surrounded and without hope. Zain spoke to the men sternly, "This man is leading you into a path of destruction. You can clearly see that you are outgunned and outmaneuvered. I suggest that we end this conflict now, preventing unnecessary bloodshed." Humiliated, the men of the band looked at one another and began to shake their heads in agreement. Defeat was clearly before them and it was time to admit it. One of the men stood up and said, "Sir, we are truly sorry for any inconvenience that we have brought upon your family, especially the two girls. We thank you for sparing our lives."

Without a word, the victors withdrew carefully, watching every move of the predators that were before them. The intruders gathered around their injured leader trying to stop the bleeding and attempting to save his hand from destruction. It was clear that the meal would be eaten in silence and would be their last in the woods as they spoke among themselves, agreeing it was time to go home.

When they were a safe distance from the fray, Zain hugged the girls and praised them for not panicking and following their training. The confiscated weapons were dispersed among the rescuers. Ammunition was not available for purchase these days and each round was precious, so the different calibers of ammunition was quickly distributed to the owners of the various calibers of rifle and the pistols and the rest was put in the Roberts family's cache to be used when necessary to defend the family again. They quietly walked out of the woods on high alert, ever mindful that over the next hill or behind the next tree could very well be an occasion to defend the family again, but happily one never came.

Dusk was now advancing as the girls approached their concealed four-wheeler and the men walked to their vehicles just over the hill, quietly slipping into the seats in the back of the truck, still mindful of any movement that was around them. With the threat over, all the time that they had practiced for such a possibility had proven successful.

When they arrived at the Roberts home and headquarters, there were hugs and tears and joy shared by all. Before the men went home to their families, Zane asked if they wanted to bow their heads and thank God for what had been provided. It was a rhetorical question, aimed more at calling the families that gathered around holding hands or hugging, and they bowed their heads in prayer. "Dear Lord, we thank you for the protection that you've given to our family. We thank you for the many hands that helped protect this family. Lord we ask that this night that you would grant us a night of rest because we know the excitement will soon overwhelm each individual and it will be hard to rest without your help. Lord we thank you for the lives that were spared and we pray Lord that one day each of these men would realize the gift of life that was before them and that they would not waste it and come to know you as their Saviour. This we ask, in the name of Jesus, Amen."

The men shook hands and quietly slipped into their vehicles to return home, knowing that if their family were in harm's way, they too could count on their extended family to join in and fight to save them. Arriving home, the men found open arms and much rejoicing from their loved ones. All were praising God for the safety that was given to the men. Each man would have a testimony of how God had intervened and saved the lives of the two young girls who were so valuable to the pastor and to his extended family.

# MELTDOWN

# Chapter 12

# Harvest and Winter

Weeks had gone by with no news involving any world altering events being broadcast. There was chatter on the short-wave radio that the Roberts family listened to hinting at a breakup of countries that would be followed by a forming of regional powers. Rumors said there would be a division of the world into ten regions that would be run by what was described as "Ten Kings." The news did not come as a shock to Zain and for the first time since the meltdown began he broke radio silence in order to verify the rumor. Sure enough, it was confirmed by one of the new regional appointees who could not remain silent. The very next morning it was reported that the man had been found unresponsive due to what they claimed was a heart attack, successfully silencing him. Pastor Zain assigned more of his home duties to his sons-in-law so that he could spend more time in his study. He could clearly identify the events taking place as end time events. The church families needed to know the timeline of the prophecies and due to the urgency of the hour, the Gospel message needed to go out before it was eternally too late.

The same week as the harvest began, word came down from the powers that be that there was an abundance of commercial harvest now available and individual families would no longer be required to turn in their excess food. They were free to can and store an unlimited amount of food. Pastor Zain was given the information to pass on to the members of the church. The local authorities recognized Zain's influence, leadership, and ability to communicate with his people and believed it best to use that resource, rather than expend the time, effort, and money to get the same information out using community leaders. Zain and Natasha felt honored to be the bearers of good news for a change! It seemed like all they ever delivered was bad news. With the phone system back in working order, precious fuel was saved as phone calls were made throughout their community. As each family was informed, a sigh of relief could be heard over the phone. They had been hoping and praying that they would not have to hide food for fear of being discovered and arrested.

That following Sunday, Pastor Zain Roberts came to the pulpit eager to preach God's Word. During the song service, Zain looked upon the faces of the singers. A burden was heavy in his heart. He knew that there were some sitting in this little country church that had not yet responded to the message of the Gospel. Their hearts had not turned to the Lord for salvation. Tears began to flow down his cheeks, for his desire, as God's Word proclaimed God's desire, was that all should repent. He knew that the heart was stubborn and some would refuse the free gift of salvation, relying instead on their own good works to save them. Stepping up to the pulpit, filled with uncertainty, knowing the days were numbered and time was growing short, Pastor Zain Roberts preached once again about the free gift of salvation and of mankind's need for a savior. With it being harvest time, he felt compelled to preach on the harvest told of in the Bible. Zain shared the news of the impending breakup of national sovereignty and of the formation of ten regions around the world. He explained to the church that the only reason this had not already occurred was because God's children still remain here. He was confident that this event would occur in the midst of the tribulation period and although they had knowledge that it was going to take place, it had not yet been announced or made official. He emphatically claimed, "No we have not been left behind!"

Services that day took on a different atmosphere as those that were saved rejoiced, but there yet remained a few that were skeptical of these events, falsely believing that the book of Revelation was metaphorical, not prophetical. Pastor Zain assured the church that this was not a time to pack their bags but a time for harvest. Physical harvest, because God could put this time on hold and they would remain here on earth together awaiting God's timetable, and spiritual harvest, because the Gospel message needed to go out to the community. They must know the truth because the Bible says, "The truth will make them free." The weight of the preaching service lifted and Zain felt that he had said all that God had called him to preach that day. At the end of the service four more precious people came forward and trusted Jesus as their Saviour.

■■■■■■■■■■■■■■■■■■■■■■■■■■■■■■■■■■■■■■■■■■■■■■■■■■■■■

At 1600 Pennsylvania Avenue in Washington, DC, it was evident that Sunday meetings had become the norm for the President's advisory team. While none of them had any religious affiliation that President James knew of, this was a day off that, instead of enjoying with family, they faithfully met to go over old news and discuss new plans. "Ladies and gentlemen," President James said, addressing his team of advisers, "Let's get this business over with so that you can spend some much needed time with your families. News reports this week indicate that there was a rumor, verified by a now deceased leader, that the world is being divided into ten regions and that each region will have an appointed leader that will answer to one world power." He paused to allow this news, including that of the deceased leader, to sink in before proceeding to further explain, "I want you to know, for health reasons, I will neither confirm, nor deny, any of those rumors." He received a few chuckles from around the room. "The official position of the White House is quite clear; we have no knowledge of any such move by any known, or unknown, world power. Do I make myself absolutely clear? Your life will depend upon it!" The president was not content with nods and a group "yea." He went around the room, person by person, confirming their agreement that they would keep this official position until informed otherwise.

With that bit of business now concluded, he proceeded to discuss the news events of the previous week. It appeared that for the first time in many months, today was filled with good news. Homeland security announced that, with trucks and trains back on the roads and rails, food was being brought into the riotous areas and that quiet was now the norm. The Secretary of Finance reported that, for the first time in several weeks, the stock market was open and trading had resumed. Reports flowed in that stocks had moved to the positive side. Leaders in the stock market anticipate that they would continue to climb and that the market would soon reach pre-reset conditions. The Secretary of Defense reported that the new peace treaties initiated had produced a complete lack of conflicts that America would need to respond to, resulting in an unprecedented peace. The Secretary of the Interior was beaming as she reported a host of new jobs repairing old bridges and roads, as well as new projects, bringing the unemployment rate of America to a record low of 3.6 percent. All indications were that this was likely to continue for the foreseeable future.

President James instructed all his advisers with positive news to make ready for the report on Monday. He would personally release this information to the White House press and pass on this great news, saying, "Ladies and gentlemen, we have finally proven that we do not need to lean on an invisible and wrathful god of this world. We have accomplished all this prosperity and peace by our own strength, resources, intelligence and good fortune. You should be proud of yourselves. History will record this day as one in which peace was in the grasp of mankind's hands. Hunger will no longer exist because countries like America, that produce an abundance of food, will be there to assist all brothers and sisters of the world with their food needs."

Later that evening President James retired to the private quarters of the White House, greeting his wife with a bouquet of flowers picked from the Rose Garden. He told her, "These are the last of the season and the staff wanted you to have them." Susan accepted the flowers, promptly handing them to a servant behind her to tend to. The election season was upon them and the American people assumed that the Jameses would be leaving this wonderful home that belongs to the people of America. Susan knew that the election would never be held and that she and her husband would be the reigning king and queen over this new region and that the seat of world power would no longer be the White House but an undisclosed fortress in Babylon. Of course, she and her husband could not breathe a word of this information, lest they find themselves in the headlines, reported as tragically killed by what the news reports would call an accident. "Jesse," she said, "I am so excited for what the future holds, and though we dare not speak publicly, indeed even privately, about what we know, my heart is heavy with what the future holds for us and this world." They exchanged a hug as if they were two teenagers with a secret that no one else knew. Post embrace, President James slipped off his tie and they adjourned to a lavish table to share their evening meal together.

With the evening services now restored, Sunday was a busy day in the Roberts family. Pulling into the driveway after the evening service was completed, Zain rejoiced, both for the new souls that were saved and for the Word of God being, once again, freely preached. Natasha had slipped out of church at the conclusion of the evening service, returning home to prepare for their traditional sandwich and game night. As she stepped onto the porch to greet her husband, she observed that his head was bowed and that he was spending time in prayer. She smiled to herself, knowing he was rejoicing in another day that men and women realized their need of a Saviour. She too rejoiced, standing silently, waiting as Zain exited his truck and walked up the steps to greet his wife. "We sure are blessed people," Natasha said, as Zain was approaching and she wrapped her arms around his neck for a much needed hug. "I don't know about you but I can hardly sleep at night knowing that any moment the Lord will return," Zain replied, "Surely God has blessed us, allowing us to serve in this day and time, observing the unfolding of the Bible before our eyes. I can hardly wait to see what He will do over these next few days, or even months, as we make ready to spend eternity with Him."

Fall turned into winter and each family of the church prepared for the cold weather ahead. Many rejoiced over their ability to heat their homes efficiently at very little cost. The harvest was over and the barns were filled to capacity allowing them to care for their livestock and feed their families. With the abundance of food and security no longer a great of concern, Zain Roberts announced to the family that they could choose to sleep above ground, and that it would be the responsibility and choice of each head of household to make that decision. "Mom and I have discussed this," Zain said, "and she has made the bedroom upstairs ready for us to sleep in tonight. Each family needs to make their own choice and I support you in any decision you make. As you know, I believe that the Lord will return soon; the Bible does not say when, but even so we will look for His return today while we plan for the work of tomorrow."

Each family member decided that they would stay until spring unless, adding with chuckles, the Lord should return before then. Winter passed without undue hardship. Ann remained free of seizures and she and Dawson joyously announced the impending birth of a new child. Kairi immediately turned to them with hugs and laughter and said, "I hope you're planning for me to be a midwife for this great event!" They replied with smiles, "We will need to see some references and we will get back to you." All the family laughed. Temperance and Kairi remained best of friends as they began to make plans for sharing a place together when they left what they affectionately called "the fortress of solitude." Temperance was excited to find a local restaurant vacant and a city eager for her to open it up so that her famous pastries could be shared by all. Kairi joined forces with a local doctor, becoming the area's traveling midwife for child birthing. Jim and Amy had managed the farm during all this and decided that they would move to the house next door. After they renovated it, making it energy efficient and off the grid as their dad had taught them, they planned to continue to run the farm they had come to love.

The first week of March arrived and the icy grip of winter was slipping into the warmer days of spring. Each family made ready for the move that they knew was coming. When the fateful morning of departure came, each family busied themselves moving their personal belongings to their new homes. Though they were not going to be far away from home, Zain and Natasha, standing on the porch arm in arm, still found it necessary to wipe away the tears that were running down their cheeks. Natasha looked up to Zain and said, "You know honey, I thought the Lord would come back before this day arrived and that we would never see our children leaving again. It sure is gonna be quiet here without the kids running around. I will miss meals shared, games played, and all the family being under one roof, even if it was covered by dirt." "Yep" was all Zain could say because he was busy holding back tears of joy.

●●●●●●●●●●●●●●●●●●●●●●●●●●●●●●●●●●●●●●●●●●●●●●●●●●●●●●

President James announced his support of his party's nominee, although he and his wife knew that the vote would never be taken. In the middle of February, President James slipped out of the White House using the secret tunnel leading to a house blocks away. He then entered an unmarked and unprotected car and made his way to the hangar where a small, unmarked jet awaited his arrival. He recognized the pilots of this flight as the same ones from his previous flights. He deduced that they knew the destination and perhaps they were even knowledgeable of the meeting that he would attend. Upon his arrival to the same secret meeting place, the doors were opened and a golf cart once again pulled up to the bottom of the stairs. Mr. James was escorted to the meeting place.

Donald Maddox, once again standing at the podium, said, "Ladies and gentlemen, this meeting will not be as lengthy as our previous meetings. Everything is now in place. In exactly one week, the United Nations general secretary will make the announcement of the world-wide treaty which all nations have signed, agreeing to abolish any and all individual constitutions in favor of a one-world constitution. He will announce that a nomination has been made for one leader of the world." Every person in the room knew this announcement would be forthcoming but they had yet to meet this nominee or hear his, or her, name. Each delegate looked around the room, wondering who this person could be. Could it be one of them that would be the nominee and called a world leader? Jesse James bubbled at the possibility that he and his wife could become the rulers of the world. The possibilities of wealth and power would be impossible to calculate. As if reading Jesse's mind, Mr. Maddox said, "I will put to rest any speculation that you may have about the possibility of being the supreme ruler of this world. This, my friends, has already been decided and the nomination and vote from the United Nations will only be a formality.

"His" name will be released at the appropriate time." The delegation members greeted one another with handshakes and hugs as Maddox departed the room and then made their way back to their respective airplanes for their journey home.

Returning unannounced and undetected to America, President James once again made his way back to the unmarked home where he would make his way through the tunnel and back into the White House, having never been missed. Of course his wife Susan knew of the trip and greeted him with open arms and squealed with joy as she heard the news that her husband delivered. After the announcement, Jesse said, "There will be a formal vote in the United Nations and our new ruler will be revealed. He will be greeted as the architect and savior of the world and will be confirmed with a unanimous vote by all countries delegates. Several months will pass, allowing the transition to be made, and protests from those so-called Christians are anticipated and will be dealt with in finality. Although many people have forgotten about it, the law that was never removed from the books will be fully implemented; religion, as we know it, will be no more."

The following week, right on schedule, the general secretary of the United Nations announced his resignation as well as the impending vote for a new world leader. The general secretary described this man as the "architect of the great Reset." The man who had placed all the nations of the world on equal footing, and "the savior" of the world. He then got down to the real information, saying, "His name is Mikhail Moretti. He is a 40-year-old single man. His father was a wealthy businessman in the European nations and his mother of Syrian dissent. He has privately met with the leader of every nation of the world and comes unanimously nominated by the nations of the world. Over the next several weeks a vote will be taken and the transfer of power will begin. Citizens of the world, we have found peace and I'm asking you to remain at peace as we come to know and love our beloved leader, Mikhail Moretti."

. . . . . . . . . . . . . . . . . . . . . . . . . . . . . . . . . . . . . . . . . . . . . . . . . . . . . . .

After hearing the announcement from the United Nations, Pastor Robert's little country church in mid-America was filled to capacity at the Wednesday night prayer meeting, not for a sermon or fellowship, but to pray, for they knew the time was short. At the Thursday evening visitation the church again filled to capacity as members paired up and canvassed their community with the news that Jesus can save IF you call upon his name. Phone calls came to the pastor's house late into the evening, as once again unprecedented numbers of people trusted Christ as our Saviour. Sunday morning, chairs needed to be set in the aisles. The windows of the auditorium were opened wide and speakers placed outside so that the crowds that had gathered could hear the preaching of the Word of God. Pastor Roberts stood up and encouraged the new believers not to be ashamed of the Gospel and to share with others the wonderful news how they had been born again. No longer did the church service last one hour, members quickly shaking hands and going home. The preaching went on for two hours and, although Zain was exhausted, the people begged for more. Zain thought to himself, could this be another great awakening that is taking place? "To God be the Glory," was all he could say. After three hours of singing, praising, and preaching, the services closed but fellowship was just beginning.

# MELTDOWN

# Chapter 13

# The Final Word

Life slowly returned to normal. Zain and Natasha said their goodbyes to their children and grandchildren as they returned to their own homes. With the civil government slowly taking charge, Zain felt it was safe to move from the protection of the underground home to their normal living space above ground permanently. Natasha spent the first few days doing a deep spring cleaning. Although the house had been maintained on a daily basis while they lived underground, she felt compelled to go room by room to make sure everything was in good order.

Surprisingly enough, it seemed as though the underground home had remained a secret, as intended. Zain spent the day visiting his church families, checking on their progress, as life returned to normal. As he was going from house to house, Zain reflected on what "normal" could be defined as. Some industrial jobs were becoming available as the power grid stabilized once again. Investors were eager to reinvest their newfound wealth with high hopes of making a profit within one year of their investments.

Zain also went to the Sheriff's Department to report the known fatalities that had occurred on his property and the premises of church members. To his surprise the sheriff gave his report little attention. Perhaps this was because his statements were very common as the final numbers were being tallied. The 90% death rate that had been predicted was not reached and for that Zain rejoiced. A new census was ordered but it had been speculated that approximately 40% of Americans did not survive the financial meltdown. With these duties concluded, Zain made his way home, knowing that dinner would soon be on the table.

A quiet dinner was shared with his wife, Natasha. As the two shared their meal together it seemed way too quiet. For the first time in many months, eating a meal alone with each other was strange. The sound of the children's voices giggling at the table as they shared jokes was missing, as was the news being shared between adults. For reasons she could not voice, Natasha sat quietly eating her meal with tears running down her cheeks. Zain asked, "What are the tears for Natasha?" She reached up, wiping her cheeks dry, and said, "For some reason it just seems too quiet!" Zain agreed that it would take some time to become accustomed to just the two of them sharing a meal again. As if a day had never been missed, Zain cleaned the table as Natasha, like other days in the past, dutifully drew the water and began to do the dishes. Zain wiped the table down and gathered their Bibles for the evening Bible study. With the Bibles out for the evening Bible study that, once again, would remind them that they were not alone, it occurred to Zain, for the first time in a long time, that he had not planned for their Bible study. When the dishes were done, Natasha came and sat down quietly, looking into the eyes of her husband. Just as she had before this mess started, Natasha began to sing a simple, but familiar song. Zain joined in. "God is so good, God is so good, God is so good, He's so good to me. He answers prayers, He answers prayers, He answers prayers, He's so good to me. I love Him so, I love Him so, I love Him so, He's so good to me." With this inspiration from his wife, Zain found it very easy to refer to the book of Psalms and so he went to Psalms 28:7 *"The LORD is my strength and my shield; my heart trusted in him, and I am helped: therefore my heart greatly rejoiceth; and with my song will I praise him."* It turned out that tonight would not be a night of Bible after all, but would be a night of praise to their Saviour, Jesus Christ. Together they spent what felt like moments but was over two hours just praising God. They reminisced about all that God had done from the very beginning. How God had directed their path in preparation for such a time as this. Tears flowed freely that evening, but they were not tears of fear, anguish, or pain. They were tears of joy, for God had been so good to them. In the final moments of their worship that night, as always, they closed in prayer. "Dear Lord," Zain prayed, "we want to thank you for being God. As other families had to say goodbye to loved ones, we have been spared that anguish. We acknowledge that it was you who gave us strength so that every day we could turn to you and know that you were beside us and this was clearly your will. We ask Lord that you watch over our family and our friends at the church over which you have placed me as the under shepherd. We ask for safety through the night as we sleep above ground. We acknowledge, as always, that it is you that has watched over us and protected us and once again we praise your Holy Name. Amen"

Zain retired to his office, as was his custom, to make notes in his personal journal about this journey of life. He looked over his notes from the last year's entry in this diary and once again was reminded that God was in control of his life, their safety, and the safety of his extended family. He picked up the pen as he had for so many years, dated the page, and began his entry of his trip to visit church families and the sheriff's office that day. He paused and reflected on the day's journey and decided, as he had in the past, to make notes and preparations for his study and preaching time. He recalled a question that was asked the first week that the meltdown of government authority took place. Many church members had asked this question and it was the first question posed to him, "Pastor, did we miss the rapture? Did we miss the time that Christ would come for his family?" they queried. Zain recalled his answer. "Just because there is a little financial hardship or hard times and persecution towards Christians does not necessarily mean that the tribulation has begun," Zain explained. "In fact, I am convinced that these times are just forerunners of the event that we Christians refer to as the rapture." The church appeared to completely accept this answer. Zain dutifully picked up his pen to make a note. Entry: Could this be the time just before the raptu . . . . .

# ABOUT THE AUTHOR

Dr. Rick Tuttle is a Navy retired enlisted veteran who was saved at the age of 15 while attending a youth rally with friends. At the age of 18 he dropped out of school and joined the Navy as an opportunity to leave the world of factory work that was his certain future. While in the Navy he completed his high school education, surrendered to preach the Gospel, and began preparing for the ministry. He stayed on active duty while attending several correspondence schools and learning the ministry through training from his pastors. He returned to Sicily where the Lord directed him and his family to start Calvary Baptist Church for the military members and their families. Accepting an early retirement, Pastor Tuttle pastored for several years in the southwest corner of Pennsylvania until accepting an appointment as pastor back in his home state of Michigan, where he currently resides. Receiving his Th.D., Dr. Tuttle turned his desire to help others into becoming a Dean of Academics in a correspondence collage, Liberty Baptist Bible College and Theological Seminary, where he continues to help men with their academics while they remain in their home churches

www.ingramcontent.com/pod-product-compliance
Lightning Source LLC
LaVergne TN
LVHW051642080426
835511LV00016B/2444